SEVEN
TIMES
AROUND

by
Bob and Ruth McKee

Banner Publishing
504 Laurel Drive
Monroeville, Pennsylvania

© 1973 by Banner Publishing
Printed in the United States of America

ISBN: 0-88368-022-X

Banner Publishing
504 Laurel Drive
Monroeville, Pennsylvania 15146
(412) 372-6420

When Jesus was preparing His disciples for the coming of the Holy Spirit, He used many descriptive phrases as an aid to their understanding. Two of these phrases were nearly always linked together as if there were a special relationship between them. "But when *The Comforter* is come . . . even the *Spirit of Truth* which proceedeth from the Father, he shall testify of me." (John 15:26).

It is the "Spirit of Truth" which enables us to be both *honest* and *real* with the Lord, ourselves and others. Such transparency of life opens us to the comforting ministry of the Holy Spirit, and also allows us to share that comfort with others in their moments of doubt and despair. (II Corinthians 1:3-6). The Psalmist beautifully expresses the foregoing truth in these familiar words which obviously were born from personal experience: "Yea, though I walk through the valley of the shadow of death, I will fear no evil for thou art with me; thy rod (protection) and thy staff (direction) they *comfort* me." We also recall in the Twenty-third Psalm that it was in the "valley" that a bountiful table was prepared, and the Lord Himself administered a special and gracious anointing.

In a very winsome way Bob and Ruth McKee lead the reader along the pathway of their lives which honestly includes the shadowed valleys as well as the sunny mountain tops. (Usually testimonies compress all of the "tops" together, and eliminate most of the "valleys." The glare of so much sunshine brings little comfort to someone in the shadows who really needs to know *how* to walk through their dark night of the soul.) I found myself moved both to tears and laughter as the McKee story progressed——perhaps because some of the road signs seemed so very familiar. But the real purpose of this little book is far more than the relating of an interesting testimony. The ways and dealings of God are presented with understanding. Principles of guidance reach forth to the reader as bright beams of truth for those who may be passing through their shadowed valley. What a comfort it is to know that others have gone before us and have found that God is indeed faithful and true to His Word.

I join my prayer with the authors' that each reader will be not only strengthened in his faith, but encouraged to remain steadfast in his calling. Undoubtedly some will discover that the Lord has brought this little book into their lives as His word to them at a most critical time. Listen carefully to what the Holy Spirit wishes to say to you for the following pages have an inspired and prophetic touch designed for your "edification, exhortation and comfort" (I Corinthians 14). Let hope, therefore, rise in your heart and blossom forth into a living faith, and you will discover as did Bob and Ruth, that the Lord truly is a Good and Faithful Shepherd!

Dr. Robert C. Frost

Author of:
Aglow in the Spirit
Life's Greatest Discovery
Set My Spirit Free

ACKNOWLEDGMENTS

We wish to thank Jan Cole and Jenny Bahr for their help in typing this book. Special thanks go to Donna Moore for typing the final manuscript, and to Rodney Lensch for his suggestions and help in proofreading.

May the Lord bless each one of our friends who had a part in the writing of this book!

Let us give thanks to the God and Father of our Lord Jesus Christ, the merciful Father, the God from whom all help comes! He helps us in all our troubles, so that we are able to help those who have all kinds of troubles, using the same help that we ourselves have received from God. (II Corinthians 1:3,4 *Good News for Modern Man*]

A close friend of ours once wrote us, "Don't forget to share your trials and testings. They're often golden nuggets." Taking this admonition to heart, we have recorded in this book a few of the mysterious, often trying, and sometimes humorous ways that God has been working in our lives. We are sharing some of these "nuggets" in the hope that they might encourage others who are going through similar experiences in their Christian walk.

Since we have been living this "new life in Christ," we have come to realize that it involves more than just expecting God to perform miracles and answer prayers. Part of God's program for helping us become mature Christians is to allow us to be subjected to trials and testings. Many Christian testimonies reflect only the mountain-top experiences. To us, it seems that Christians should share some of their valley experiences as well. This is where we meet "the Lily of the Valley" and where the roots grow deepest. As the writer of Hebrews put it, "All discipline for the moment seems not to be joyful, but sorrowful; yet to those who have been trained by it, afterwards it yields the peaceful fruit of righteousness." [Hebrews 12:11 *New American Standard Bible*]

Contents

TO OUR CHILDREN
STEVE, DANNY, DAVID, TONI

1

Encounter

"Ruth, I feel like something really good is going to happen to me." These were the words I shared with my wife as we began the year in 1962. I had been seeking and searching for reality of life for several months before this because of internal frustrations, fears and discontentment. In May of 1962 something did happen that completely and dramatically changed my life and gave me the peace I was searching for.

Bob speaking:

We were an average American family consisting of myself, Ruth, the three boys, Steve, Danny, David and a girl, Toni. We were respected and respectable members of St. Paul's Episcopal Church in Pomona, California. For us adult McKees, the "good life" was to do the town in Hollywood on Saturday night, or possibly make it to Las Vegas for a week-end. We were active in Little League Baseball, the P.T.A., and our church—but something was missing. That something (we found out later) was God. We were missing the mark. Is it possible for an active church-goer to be missing a personal relationship with God? We can answer from our own experience that it is.

That we even attended church was somewhat surprising, since neither of us was brought up in a church-going family. My parents believed in God, but only in a very abstract way. Their attitude—and mine—was that He was there only for our convenience when we were in trouble and needed help. One of the first occasions on which I needed (and definitely received) His help came about in World War II.

I was the radioman on a torpedo plane aboard a carrier in the South Pacific. Our mission was to support ground troops fighting in the various Japanese-held islands. Each time we were to be catapulted into the air for another strike, I would plead with God for a safe return. Then, as soon as the plane had jerked to a halt on the deck of the carrier, I would forget about Him until the next flight was scheduled. I know now that, even though I forgot about Him, He never forgot about me.

During the battle for Iwo Jima, anti-aircraft fire hit our plane, damaging the control system and puncturing the fuel tank so that the gasoline came back into the radio compartment where I sat. To avoid being overcome by the fumes, I put on my oxygen mask. The pilot realized that we wouldn't be able to make it back to the carrier and decided to ditch in the ocean. Fearing that the eight rockets still under the wings of the plane would explode as we crash landed, he shot them off. As the rockets were launched, sheets of flame shot back four or five feet. What kept the gasoline from catching fire, only God knows.

Although I was semi-conscious as a result of the fumes and the impact of the crash landing, I realized I was standing knee deep in water. The seat I was sitting on was still strapped to me as it had ripped loose during the crash. Being groggy and dazed, I was not too coherent so my gunner had to instruct me to release the straps holding me in the seat. After having gotten out himself he then began helping me up through the top turret.

As I fell out onto the wing of the plane, which was partly submerged in the water I attempted to inflate my life jacket. I heard air escaping and I knew that the air chambers in my jacket were torn. Swimming around in the water I could see that both my gunner and pilot were safe. The pilot had gotten the life raft out of the plane and it was inflated so I swam to it. With his help and a few moments of struggle, I fell into the raft.

We were in the water just a short time when a destroyer escort picked us up. On the deck of the rescue ship I began spitting up something green. I thought sure I had ruptured my insides until someone told me it was marker dye that had spilled into the water from the crash. I had swallowed a good amount of the Pacific Ocean and the dye was in it. It did not make me sick, only concerned for a short time. When

I asked the pilot how long the plane had stayed afloat he said about three minutes. Yes, God was looking after me even though I called on Him only when in need.

Ruth and I had grown up just two blocks from each other in Webster Groves, Missouri, and had been friends since we were 11 years old. When I was discharged from the service in 1946, we decided to get married. Because of the influence of her grandmother, Ruth was more concerned about religion than I was.

When we began making plans for our marriage, Ruth found out I had not been baptized. "Bob, you will have to be baptized, so that you can go to heaven," she told me. I replied that I didn't want to stand up in front of all those people in church and make a spectacle of myself. Her answer was, "Bob, if you want to marry me, you will have to be baptized." So, at the age of 21, I was baptized in the First Presbyterian Church of Webster Groves. John the Baptist had a baptism, and so did Ruth. I was baptized into "Ruth's baptism." There was no repentance in my heart, and I did not do it to please God but to please Ruth. Again I was only using God to satisfy my needs.

After we were married, we became C&E (Christmas and Easter) Christians, attending church about twice a year. As our family increased, I gave less and less thought to God. In 1955—partly because of a growing restlessness within us—we moved to Pomona, California, where I worked in construction as an electrician. I still was not interested in going to church, but Ruth began visiting the Episcopal Church on Sunday mornings. She soon started asking me to go with her, but I always had an excuse. One Sunday she said, "Bob, if you are not concerned with your own soul, then neither will I be." Somehow that remark struck home, and from that time on I began attending church regularly with her.

In time we took confirmation instructions and became increasingly active members of St. Paul's Episcopal Church. Within a few years, I was junior warden on the Vestry (the governing body of the church) and was serving on many committees. Ruth was on the library committee and our three boys were acolytes. We presented the picture of a respectable Christian family, but we both knew that something was still very, very wrong. Church activities had not provided the fulfillment we were looking for. Even during the Sunday-morning services of worship, my mind was on anything and everything but God. I thought Communion in itself would fill the void, and I would try to look pious as I came back from the Communion rail. I was wearing my mask of righteousness, but inside I was empty.

Ruth and I were members of the Adult Discussion Class, a group that met on Sunday morning after the 9 o'clock service to discuss anything from soup to nuts—usually not too much about God. Since the discussions invariably introduced more problems than solutions, we re-labeled the group the "Adult Confusion Class."

On a memorable Sunday morning in May of 1962, I was standing in the hall—not wanting to go into the confusion class. One of those "strange people" in our church who spoke in tongues and went to prayer meetings on Saturday nights also "happened" to be standing there, and I began talking to her. Although I had struck up a conversation with Jane this morning about those "fanatics" it was not the first time I had been affected by them. Two years earlier, our church had held a Parish Life Conference over a week-end, during which about 40 of us came together to discuss the Christian approach to life. It was during this conference that Ruth and I first came into contact with people who did strange and different things like speaking in tongues.

My first experience came in a small "buzz group." While we were deep in discussion, one of the women in the group began speaking in a language that was foreign to me and, I believe, to the others as well. A very strange feeling came upon me—a sort of awesome fear of God. One of my legs wanted to get up and go, and the other wanted to stay. I finally decided that what was happening couldn't be too bad, since we were in an Episcopal Church and the one speaking was an Episcopalian!

When Ruth and I met again in the large group, I told her what had happened. She was excited about it and wished she could have heard the woman speaking in tongues. It wasn't long before she had the opportunity—for another woman in the large group did the same thing. After the conference broke up that evening, Ruth said, "Let's go into the sanctuary and pray." My answer was, "Forget it. I'm afraid the same thing will happen to us that happened to those women."

As I talked with Jane that Sunday morning two years later, I tried tactfully to find out what was different about her and her fellow "fanatics," but she would volunteer no more information than I asked for. I believe she was given wisdom from God to force nothing on me, because her reticence whetted my curiosity. As we ended the conversation, she gave me a magazine called *Trinity*. I took it home and put it on the coffee table, but didn't look at it during the rest of the day. Little did I know that I had brought the magazine home for Ruth to read.

After I left for work the next day, Ruth picked up the magazine and began to glance through it. One of the articles that impressed her was by Dennis Bennett, who wrote about receiving something called "the baptism in the Holy Spirit" while he was rector of a large Episcopal Church in Van Nuys, California. In addition to his testimony, this issue contained those of several laymen who had received the same sort of "baptism." One thing they all agreed upon was that this experience had transformed their lives and made Jesus Christ a living reality to each of them. For them, Christianity had become an exciting, vibrant way of life instead of a ho-hum responsibility. Ruth couldn't put the magazine down until she had read all of the articles. A real excitement was building up in her, and she knew they had something she wanted.

2

I Know That I Know That I Know

Ruth speaking:

Although my parents had never attended church when I was growing up, there always seemed to be within me a hunger to know more about God. In my late teens my sister and I joined a Presbyterian church a few blocks from our home. We attended there for about three years off and on. I still remember the beautiful Christmas Eve services but we did not find any real reality in Jesus Christ.

Even though I insisted on Bob's being baptized before we were married, we seldom attended church thereafter, except to have our three boys baptized. I began having problems with my health and my nerves after the birth of our first son. During my third pregnancy I was given tranquilizers, which seemed to help me feel much more relaxed. We moved to California when our third son was three years old, and my doctor there began telling me I should stop taking the tranquilizers. Although I ignored his warning, I began attending the Episcopal Church in Pomona—perhaps partly with the hope of finding there the real tranquility that I was seeking in pills. With the birth of our little girl a year later, however, I felt under more pressure than ever before and I relied more and more on my pills.

There were times when I felt I would simply come unglued unless I could get away from the children for a night out. So at least once a month Bob and I would go to a bang-up party or a night club. We had a good time; but the release from tension was only temporary. After Bob and the children began going to church with me, we found somewhat more lasting satisfaction in church activities—but still I did not have peace. Christmas cards with all those nice sayings about peace began to bug me. Where was this "peace on earth, good will toward men" that they talked about? Although we attended church every Sunday now, observed the Lenten tradition, and fasted (not eating after midnight) before Communion, we still had no real peace. The benediction given by our priest each Sunday contained beautiful words about God's peace—but I was not experiencing that peace.

In 1961 I came across a copy of Lillian Roth's autobiography, *I'll Cry Tomorrow*, which paints a vivid picture of her degrading life as an alcoholic. As I read her story, the sobering thought came to me: "Ruth, you are as bound to tranquilizers as she was to drink." Badly as this realization frightened me, the thought of not having my pills was even more terrifying.

I used to count them to make sure I wouldn't run out over a week-end. Our drug bills every year were enormous!

Shortly after Lillian Roth's book had opened my eyes to my drug-dependency, Dr. Norman Vincent Peale's book *The Power of Positive Thinking* came into my hands. One verse of Scripture quoted in that book spoke to me plainly: *"I can do all things through Christ which strengtheneth me."* [Philippians 4:13] Inspired by this Scripture, I took a step of faith and ground up all my pills in the garbage disposal. Instead of a pill, I put this verse of Scripture in my mouth several times a day and each night at bedtime, saying it out loud or to myself.*

The first few days weren't easy, but I determined to see it through. Gradually I began to feel better and better, and my thinking pattern began changing from one of fear and negativism to a more positive one.

When I went back to my doctor for a checkup three or four months later, my blood pressure was normal for the first time in years and there was no evidence of any of my former health problems. I didn't know enough at that time to exclaim "Praise the Lord!" Instead I gave the credit to my "positive thinking." When I met the living God several months

---

*In sharing this experience, I never encourage anyone to dispose of his medicine unless the Lord has spoken to his heart. Drug-dependency can't be broken on the basis of someone else's faith; it must be your own.

later, I said humbly, "Oh God, you touched me that day I ground up my pills. You honored that step of faith, and now I give You the glory." God set me free from the pills and healed me physically even before I experienced spiritual healing.

After this experience of deliverance and physical healing, I realized increasingly that our adult class at church spent much more time tearing the Scriptures apart than really searching for the truth in them. Believing only the parts of Scriptures that appealed to our own intellect, we had a tape-and-scissors version of the Bible: we taped in what suited our way of thinking and cut out the parts we didn't agree with. I became more and more confused and began to reason within myself that either the Bible was true or it wasn't. How could I believe one part and not another? If one part wasn't true, then why should I believe that any of it was? Either Jesus and His words were true, or they weren't.

I began to hunger spiritually as never before. My heart was open and searching now. One day I went to my bedroom, got down on my knees, and cried out to God for reality. "Oh God, if You are really real, if You do exist, please make Yourself real to me, so that I may *know!* Give me some tangible experience, so I'll know that I know that I know!" God heard that call for help and the cry of my heart to draw near to him. It was about a month later that Bob had his conversation with Jane and brought home the magazine that she gave him.

In the past I had actually crossed the street to avoid meeting those persons from our parish who attended a Saturday-night prayer meeting. My thinking was, "Baptists go to prayer meetings, but not Episcopalians. What on earth do they *do* there?" I had all sorts of questions in my mind about these people, and I was upset when Bob talked to Jane during our coffee time after church. I wondered why he wanted to carry on a conversation with those "kooky people." We were a respectable, dignified Episcopalian family, and I wanted to keep it that way!

I don't know what led me to pick up the magazine that Bob had dropped on the coffee table —but once I had opened it, my Monday-morning chores were completely forgotten. As I read testimony after testimony by men and women who had entered a new dimension of Christian living after receiving the baptism in the Holy Spirit, I felt my excitement mounting. I *knew* that these people had found what I was seeking, and my only question was, "Lord, where can I get in on this? Where? *Where?*"

The following Friday in the religious section of our local newspaper I saw that the editor of the magazine that I had just read would be speaking at a Foursquare Church in a nearby community. I had never heard of a Foursquare Church before, and wondered why she couldn't speak in an Episcopalian or at least a Presbyterian Church! I rarely ever even glanced at the religious section of the newspaper up until this time! The next Sunday morning at St. Paul's, forgetting both pride and prejudice, I mentioned having seen the article in the paper to Jane. She invited Bob and I to attend the meeting that night with her and offered to pick us up. We told her we would call before 7:00 p.m. and let her know for sure if we wanted her to come by to pick us up. I was really looking forward to going now, but Bob wasn't too enthusiastic and by 6:30 had decided he did not care to go. I was somewhat frustrated then as I had wanted him to go along and now I had to decide whether to go without him or not go at all. I kept watching the clock and had not called Jane back. By 7:00 p.m. I exclaimed, "God, do something. If you are in all of this have Jane call me." I was startled to hear the phone ring immediately. It was Jane asking whether we wanted her to come by or not and I said, "Yes, please do." Jane was very disappointed when she arrived to find out that Bob had decided to stay home and only I would be going with her. She felt that Bob had been more open to receive her witness than I had been.

The service that Sunday night was, to say the least, very different from our services at St. Paul's. Yet as I heard the testimony of all that God was doing, I knew in my inmost being that those who testified were in touch with the risen Christ. At the conclusion of the service, they sang a hymn I'd never heard before; "Spirit of the Living God, Fall Afresh on Me." And He certainly did! I didn't know that I was sitting with a row full of Spirit-filled Episcopalians who had been praying for me for a couple of months. No wonder I felt so much power or that I responded to the invitation to go to the prayer room!

As I left my seat, my heart was beating rapidly. I was both excited and apprehensive about what might be going on in the prayer room. I wouldn't have been surprised to see people rolling on the floor or swinging from the chandeliers. Although nothing so outlandish took place, a woman was crying when I entered. We didn't cry at St. Paul's, and so I began to freeze up. Our assistant rector once quipped, "The Hebrews were God's chosen people; we Episcopalians are God's *frozen* people." That described me perfectly—and although those who were ministering in the prayer room laid hands on me and prayed, I remained *frozen*.

Before leaving church to go home, Jane asked if she and some of our fellow Episcopalians could stop in to pray for Bob and me together that evening. Although I was thinking "No" inside, I nodded my head "Yes." They arrived about 10 and stayed until after 1, sharing with us all that God was doing in their lives through the power of His Spirit. They talked to us of Jesus as if He were a personal Friend, and told us how to receive the promise of the Holy Spirit. Then they prayed for us both—and still nothing seemed to happen.

Within me, however, a cleansing had begun. I spent most of the next day weeping and praying. My longing for God and His fullness in my life became so great that on Tuesday morning I called Jane and asked her to take me back to that Foursquare Church and ask the minister to pray for me. (That minister, Chuck Smith, later became a dear friend of ours and held Bible studies in our home for almost a year.) While I was waiting for Jane to come, I went into my bedroom to pray again and asked God not to let me get mixed up in anything that wasn't of Him. With my eyes closed, I opened my prayer book at random and put my finger down on the page. When I opened my eyes, I found that I had turned to the hymns for Whitsuntide (Pentecost) and my finger was on the words, "Come, Thou Holy Spirit, come."

With this assurance that I was on the right track, I walked back into the living room and asked God to fill me with the Holy Spirit. Then, in faith, I opened my mouth as I had been instructed previously. In my mind was the thought, "If God be God and if He parted the Red Sea, raised the dead, and caused a virgin to conceive, it can't be too hard for Him to give me a language of worship and praise." With that I began to speak and heard a beautiful language begin to pour out of my mouth—and I mean *pour!* As it rolled out, in my understanding I was saying, "Oh, it's real, it's real, it's *real!*" The Spirit made me so aware of the presence of Jesus that I felt as though He had laid His hand on my forehead and said, "You're mine; you are sealed with My Holy Spirit of promise." The assurance of my salvation now flooded my entire being. I had passed from death unto Life. There was no more fear of dying; I knew in my heart that I would see Jesus face to face! Then a great peace seemed to fill me to overflowing. Here at last was that peace I had longed for— the peace of God which "passeth all understanding." [Philippians 4:7] It was more than beautiful words in a benediction; it was a tangible experience which let me know beyond the shadow of a doubt that peace is in a Person, and that Person is Jesus!

When Jane came to pick me up, she found me crying softly, laughing, and dancing around the living room all at once. I wasn't exactly a "respectable, dignified Episcopalian" at that time! Rejoicing together, we drove to Chuck's church and shared with him the tremendous thing that had happened to me. As the three of us offered our worship and praise to God, I suddenly realized that my personal Pentecost had come just five days before Whitsunday. Never again would that Sunday be for me just the day when the color of the altar cloth was changed from white to red!

3

Touching the Hem
of His Garment

Bob speaking:

On the day that Jesus baptized Ruth in the Holy Spirit, she met me at the door as I came home from work. Before she said a word, I knew something had happened to her. There was a radiance coming forth as her face glowed like a light. As she joyfully tried to share her experience and her excitement with me, my only comment was, "Let me hear you speak in the Language God gave you!" There was no love in my voice, and I said it in a challenging way.

To tell the truth, I was sort of mad at what had taken place. I thought to myself, "Here I'm the one who talked to Jane and brought home the magazine, and God gave this to Ruth first!" Although I wasn't sure what she had received, I knew I wanted whatever it was. For the rest of the week there was a real gulf between us. The happier she got the more miserable I became.

One evening during the week Ruth went to hear a speaker that was talking about the work of the Holy Spirit. She had gone with several people from our church that had also received the Baptism in the Holy Spirit. When she came home she was just bubbling over with joy. She began sharing with me what went on at the meeting and how happy and joyful the people were that attended. The more she talked, the more it upset me. Soon I found myself trying to pop her bubble and when I didn't succeed went off to bed in a huff! Ruth quickly learned not to share any more with me unless I asked questions. Even though she didn't share in words, the joy of the Lord still remained evident.

The following Saturday night we were invited to the prayer meeting that Ruth had viewed with much suspicion. As we were on our way to the Bakers' home, where it was being held, I wondered anxiously what I was letting myself in for. When we arrived, I chose a seat in the corner of the room so that I could observe the proceedings and stay out of the way. Soon the room was filled with wall-to-wall people. The meeting was very different from any I had been to before. After the group had sung some choruses that I didn't know and that didn't sound like any hymns I had learned in church, various individuals began praying to Jesus as though He were in the center of the room. Then something even stranger was done. John Baker sat a chair out and invited those who wanted prayer to come and sit in the "hot seat" as others laid hands on them and prayed with them. This was almost too much for me. If I could have gotten out of my corner, I would have left the meeting but fast! I had thought I was playing it smart to sit in a corner away from the center of activities, but I was actually playing right into God's hand: I couldn't leave, because I was boxed in.

As John continued to invite people to come forward for prayer, he would look at me and grin from ear to ear. I was feeling mighty uncomfortable by this time and kept telling myself, "He is not going to get me up in that chair in front of all those people. I am not about to make a spectacle of myself for anyone." My mind was made up (I thought), but God knew my heart and the hunger in it. He had a better idea. While the praying continued, a young man entered the room and soon began speaking in an unknown tongue. As the room instantly became quiet, I heard God speak to my heart. From another person came the interpretation of the tongue, and I knew it was God speaking right to me. In essence He was saying "That void in your life is because I am missing, come to me tonight and I will fill it with my love." Almost before I realized it, I was out of my corner and sitting in the "hot seat." Then the strangest thing of the evening was happening to me: I found myself crying like a baby—and I didn't even care!

You know, we men have a "thing" about crying: we feel that it causes us to lose our masculinity. I used to think it was OK to swear a lot if I banged my finger with a hammer, since this kept up the masculine image—but I would never be caught crying! How phony can we get? God made tears a natural vent for our emotions of hurt, grief, and joy. I had found Joy this night, because I knew that Jesus had come into my life, and I didn't care who saw me cry! Something else changed for me also: the name of the chair. Instead of a "hot seat," it became a "mercy seat"—because that's what I found there.

Several in the room gathered around me and asked if I wanted to receive the Baptism in the Holy Spirit. By this time I wanted everything and anything God would give me. They told me to ask Jesus to baptize me with the Holy Spirit, and then to expect Him to give me a new language of praise. The Lord said that we should come to Him in simple faith and trust, as a little child. This I did as I asked Jesus for the promise of the Father. Then I began to praise Him in English—and other syllables came forth that I didn't understand. Instead of letting the strange language flow out, I was so surprised that I stopped speaking. Those that had gathered around me to pray continued to encourage me to have more fluency in my new language, but nothing more seemed to happen. Since it was almost 2:30 a.m., the meeting soon broke up.

Many times in the past Ruth and I had come home late on Saturday night full of spirits. This Saturday night, for the first time, we came home filled with the Spirit of God. Our oldest son,

31

Steve, had been serving as our baby-sitter and was still awake when we got home. Ruth saw that he got to bed and then checked the other three children before coming to bed herself. As we knelt to pray, we reached across the bed and held hands; then, for the first time in my presence, Ruth began speaking in the language God had given her. This must have unlocked the floodgates of heaven inside me, because my language burst forth in a torrent of praise! The more I spoke, the faster and louder the words came. It felt as if I had been lifted up from my bedroom floor to a place next to Jesus, and had touched the hem of His garment. My worshipping became so noisy that it woke Steve. As Ruth went in to reassure him, he said, "That's Dad talking, but what's wrong with him?" Ruth assured him that I was all right; but since she was crying and laughing for joy at what God had done for me, it was hard for her to convince him. Before we finally got to sleep about 5 a.m., we had both gone into Steve's bedroom that he shared with our second son, Danny. We sat on the bed and tried to explain all that had happened. Steve said that he had first thought I was sick as he thought I was moaning, but then he realized it was this religious thing we had been discussing. Steve soon fell asleep, but Ruth and I were too excited for sleep right then.

What a change came into our lives after that night! What was once a puzzle to read now became food for the soul. We wanted to devour the complete Bible from cover to cover all at once. We hated to go to bed at night, because we were afraid God was going to do something and not tell us about it! As the love of Jesus began building up inside of me, I felt as if someone were pumping up my heart with a tire pump—until it seemed that it would burst in my chest. Reluctantly, I asked God to take some of His love away; so much of it at one time was just more than I could stand! I soon realized that I prayed amiss. I should have asked God to increase the capacity of my heart to contain the love He was pouring in. I also know now why we will have to have glorified bodies when we see Jesus face to face in all His splendor.

Even after the Lord stopped pumping love into my heart, our life had a new and vibrant meaning now that the Holy Spirit was in charge. For the first time we could see a real purpose for our existence. No longer did I wonder, "Who am I?" "Why am I here?" "Where am I going when I die?" These questions had been answered in a way that removed all doubt. We looked forward to each new day with real excitement, wondering what God had in store for us. Our values, priorities, and interests were radically changed, and things that were at one time of utmost importance in our lives now became secondary.

A few years before our encounter with Jesus, Ruth and I went with some of our friends to see the film *South Pacific*. For several weeks afterward, we all dreamed of living on an island in the tropics. Since that seemed to be out of the question, Ruth and I tried to escape from the pressures of our daily existence by frequent week-end trips to Hollywood or Las Vegas. Sure we had fun—but when the excitement wore off, we found ourselves again caught in the same old rat race. Little did we know at the time that the problem was within us, and *we couldn't run away from ourselves*. It would not have mattered where we went or what we did to try to satisfy this unrest. Without God to fill this void in our lives, we would have remained empty, purposeless, and out of kilter.

Praise God, we finally found the real thing! No more did we need to turn to a make-believe world in an effort to escape from the pressures of the real one. Now we had an inner peace that only Jesus Christ can give—a peace which doesn't depend on circumstances. In his letter to the Philippians (4:7), Paul called it "the peace of God, which passeth all understanding." Man can try every other avenue looking for this peace: he may gain the wealth of the world; he may attain the highest position in his profession; he may move to the most romantic and appealing place on earth. But unless he meets the living God, his inner restlessness will never be stilled. Man was made for God, and his inner drive will not be satisfied until he establishes fellowship through Jesus Christ. No more did we have to search and look for that cloud with the silver lining. We had found the Creator of the Cloud and had met Him in a personal way!

4

Experiences with a
Home Prayer Meeting

Bob speaking:

Several months before our encounter with
Christ and our Baptism in the Holy Spirit,
Ruth and I had picked out a lovely
home which was under construction in Upland, California. When we first saw the large
living room, we envisioned lively parties there.
(A former neighbor of ours once told us that
we had the noisiest parties in the neighbor-
hood.) Shortly after entering into our new relationship with Jesus, we went to Upland to
check on the progress of the building. When we
walked into that large room again, we looked
at each other and exclaimed, "Oh, what prayer
meetings we can hold here! Praise the Lord!"

That's exactly what happened. We had lively
gatherings in that living room, all right; but the
Life of the "parties" was the Holy Spirit. Within
a week or so after our move, from Pomona,
while bedspreads and sheets still hung over the
windows in the place of drapes, Chuck Smith,
the pastor of the Foursquare Church in Los
Serrentos, began holding a weekly Bible study

in our home. We have always been grateful to him for giving us a solid foundation in the Scriptures and teaching us the importance of staying grounded in the Word. Many of those who attended the Bible studies in our home were, like Ruth and me, spiritually hungry but painfully ignorant about the Bible.

After teaching us for almost a year, Chuck moved to Costa Mesa; but for two more years our home was open every Saturday night for a prayer meeting and Bible study. Many servants of God came into our home during these years to teach, share and commune with us; and people from many different denominations came there to worship and pray together. Some found Christ as Savior at these meetings; many received the Holy Spirit in His fullness; others were healed. We had potluck suppers with wonderful fellowships. One time the Cameron family from Scotland was there—and it was quite a Happening!

Home prayer meetings afford an opportunity for "babes in Christ" to learn from more mature Christians how to wait upon the Lord, how to develop spiritual gifts, and how to pray and worship. In this atmosphere of informality, freedom, and love, even staid Lutherans and Episcopalians begin to come out of their shells of inhibition and to share with others. As they pray for one another's needs, they begin to understand what Body ministry is and to experience the fellowship of the Holy Spirit that is found only in a living organism which is part of the Body of Christ. Home prayer groups are an integral part of God's plan, and purpose for His people although they do not take the place of a church. Those who attend home meetings should also be attached to a local church. Everyone, including the leader of the group, should have a pastor.

"Believe Not Every Spirit"

One of the things God is developing and desiring in home prayer groups is good leadership. Just having a home large enough for meetings is not the important thing. I believe that when a home is opened for Christian fellowship, the man of the house should assume leadership, functioning as an elder or under-shepherd and guarding his "flock" against false teaching and evil influences.

We learned very quickly that as our doors were opened to God's people, Satan came in also. God does not want us to remain spiritual babes. Some of the Pentecostals who came to the meetings in our home wanted to "set us straight" bringing more law than liberty; others wanted to sell their pet doctrines; and still others were in cults. God was showing us that we were not to be naive about spiritual matters. Jesus warned His disciples (Matthew 10:16) to be "wise as serpents and harmless as doves." We learned not to accept all tongues, interpretation, and prophecy that came forth in a meeting as being anointed of God. Even if a prophecy ended with "Thus saith the Lord," it was to be judged!

I believe the Lord allowed us to be exposed to most of the false teachings in these first three years of fellowship. We heard everything —from elaborate expositions by those who believed they had reached a state of sinless perfection and would never experience physical death to prophecies of doom by a frustrated woman who thought she was a prophetess of God. This woman attended our meetings quite often. There seemed to be a heavy cloud over the meeting when she was there, and most of her sharing brought condemnation on the group.

One evening a young woman named Linda asked for prayer. As she sat in the "prayer chair" for ministry, the self-appointed prophetess came up to pray for her. As she laid hands on her, Linda cried out with real fear in her voice. After the meeting was over, we talked with Linda and asked her what had happened. She said that when the woman's hands touched her, she felt an evil presence and a definite sense of depression, which had remained. We prayed with her until the depression lifted and a peace settled upon her.

As leader of the meetings held in our home, I felt that I was responsible to God and to all present for what took place and that I could not allow this kind of thing to continue. Phoning the pastor of the woman who brought the problems into the meetings, I told him what had happened and asked him to talk to her about this matter. I explained that we thought it would be best for her not to come back to the meetings until she had changed her attitude. The pastor was very understanding and said she had caused nothing but trouble in his church, bringing forth false prophecies and making suggestions to him which he knew were not of the Lord. He agreed to talk with her, and she did not come back to our home again.

Even though Ruth and I were still relatively ignorant of Scripture and made many mistakes in our conduct of the meetings in our home, God was with us. When someone introduced a false doctrine, the Lord would reveal it to Ruth, to me, or to one of the more mature Christians in the group. Their prayers and their counsel often prevented Satan from detouring us.

Dr. Robert Frost was one of the spiritual leaders who taught our prayer group on occasion, and he made a comment that has stuck in my mind: "Satan always overplays his hand. Listen closely to what is being said and to what is not being said, and notice what the speaker does with Jesus."

"The Lighter Side"

Ruth speaking:

As we continued with our meetings, many humorous things occurred—or things that seem humorous in retrospect. At the time they happened, we were not amused!

At one meeting, a member of the group whispered into my ear as she entered the house, "I hope you don't mind, but we have brought a man who is involved in spiritualism." I could hardly believe what I had heard! Immediately I passed the information on to Bob—but because several had entered the house at the same time, I wasn't sure which one was the spiritualist.

As the meeting proceeded, we noticed a white-haired man sitting next to the person who had spoken to me. We thought, "He must be the one." Remembering Jesus' promise to His disciples that "Whatsoever ye shall bind on earth shall be bound in Heaven" (Matthew 18:18), we began silently to bind this man so that he couldn't bring forth his teaching. The meeting continued all evening without the slightest comment from him.

After the meeting was over, we were introduced to the man involved in spiritualism—and found that he was not the one we had bound! The "bound" man later became a good friend of ours, and we were able to laugh together at the comedy of errors.

On another night a teenage girl, a member of a local Pentecostal church, was brought to the prayer group by two Pentecostal women who wanted us to pray for her to "receive the Holy Ghost." During the time of ministry we asked the girl whose name I do not remember so I will call her Susie to sit in the prayer chair in the middle of the room. Several members of the group prayed for her, but nothing seemed to happen. Bob then suggested that I take her into our bedroom and pray for her privately. Her two friends insisted on accompanying us, and while I was instructing and encouraging Susie they were pacing back and forth loudly beseeching God to let His power fall and fill her with His Spirit. I was wishing they would tone it down a bit, since it was now 11 p.m. and the Episcopal dean of the San Bernardino Convocation and his wife lived next door. Their bedroom window was directly across from ours, and our window was open.

Finally Susie opened her mouth and gave voice to the promptings of the Holy Spirit. As the power of God fell upon her, she began to tremble and then to speak in tongues and weep at the same time. Soon she was praising God in tongues loud and clear while her two friends, now with their hands in the air, continued to pace the room shouting "Glory to God! Hallelujah! GLORY!" I must admit that my rejoicing was tempered with thoughts of our next-door neighbors' reaction!

As Susie kept getting louder and more tearful, I began to be afraid that she was becoming too emotional. Not knowing exactly what to do, I said to her, "Honey, you certainly have received the Holy Spirit—no doubt about that! Now, how would you like some punch and cookies?" She didn't reply but continued to weep and shout. I thought, "Oh, no! Maybe she *can't* stop! Please, Lord Jesus, turn it off!" After

41

that brief but heartfelt prayer, I tried again: "Honey, we have nice cold punch in the kitchen and lots of good cookies. How would you like some?" Again no reply.

In desperation, I ran into the living room to get help. Finding my husband, I drew him aside and whispered urgently, "Bob, please come help me! I can't get the girl to stop speaking in tongues and quiet down. Her two friends are about to shout the roof off, and the dean must be able to hear all this next door!" Bob went back into the bedroom with me and began to talk to Susie. After he finally got her quieted, her two friends stopped their pacing and shouting and things became calm again.

This was the first time we had to quiet anyone down. The person speaking in tongues always has full control of the volume that comes forth, and most people have to be encouraged to speak out. This incident taught us that there can be a time to urge self-control as well as a time to encourage release.

5

The Power of God to Heal

Bob speaking:

During the first few years after Ruth and I were filled with the Holy Spirit it seemed that almost every prayer we offered received an immediate affirmative answer. A young Baptist layman called me one day to ask me to pray for Charles, a 17-year-old youth who had taken an overdose of sleeping tablets in an attempt at suicide; he said the boy was in a coma and was not expected to live. I told him I would ask God to show me whether He wanted me to go to the hospital to pray for Charles, and whether others were to go with me. As I was in prayer about the matter, the doorbell rang. A Lutheran member of our prayer group and close friend, Don Brown, had come to pick up his daughter, who was visiting our daughter Toni. I told him about the situation and asked him to seek God's guidance about going with me to the hospital. About 15 minutes later, Don called to say that he would meet me there in a few minutes.

At the hospital we met Charles' father and explained to him our desire to pray for his son.

He was very appreciative but said that his boy was in the Intensive Care Unit, where only his parents were allowed to see him for brief periods. Our reply was, "If God wants us to pray for him, the door will be opened." The father then went to the nurse in charge of the unit and told her what we wanted to do. She offered no objection and asked only that we put on hospital gowns and masks and that we not touch the patient. After donning the required attire, we entered the Intensive Care Unit with Charles' father and went to the bed where his son lay unconscious. I prayed first in English and then in the language God had given me. Don prayed in the same way, and then Charles' father said a short prayer in English. As we left the room, Don and I were completely confident that our prayers had been heard. (How great it is to pray and to be given an assurance in your heart! Praying in the Spirit can allow you to feel this way.)

Soon after reaching home, I received a phone call from our Baptist friend telling me that Charles had already begun to regain consciousness. A few days later he was released from the hospital, completely healed. We learned later that Charles had swallowed his tongue while unconscious, and that his brain had been without oxygen for a few minutes. The doctors had given him up to die and said that if he were to live he would be a vegetable. God sovereignly performed a miracle and restored him so com-

pletely that he was later inducted into the
army.

"Two Miracles for Peggy"

Ruth speaking:
One Wednesday morning, as I was ironing, I
received a phone call from Gwen, a member of
our prayer group who had been miraculously
healed of diabetes a few years earlier. She
wanted me to go with her to pray for a friend
of hers named Peggy, who was in such intense
pain from a terminal cancer of the stomach that
she had not slept for several nights. After I
agreed to go, I hung up the phone thinking, "I
sure hope Gwen is prayed up, because I'm not
feeling too spiritual." When Gwen came to pick
me up about ten minutes later, her first words
were, "Ruth, I hope you are in tune with God
this morning." I replied, "Oh no, Gwen! I was
hoping *you* were!" With a deep sense of our in-
adequacy, we prayed *hard* all the way to Peggy's
home. There we met Barbara, a neighbor of Peggy's who had recently received the baptism in
the Holy Spirit.

Peggy was sitting in a chair, doubled over
with pain. Gwen asked her if she believed God
could heal her. Although not an active church
member, Peggy had attended the Catholic
Church as a child and she replied in the affirmative. Then the three of us—an Episcopalian, a member of the Assembly of God, and a
Southern Baptist—gathered around Peggy to

45

pray. Acting in one accord, this ecumenical group laid hands on her and, in the power of Jesus' name, came against the cancer. Almost immediately Peggy exclaimed, "It's gone! Oh, it's all gone! Oh, thank you, God, *thank* you! It's gone!" The pain that had been racking her body had suddenly ceased, and she was able to sit upright in the chair. All four of us had an awesome awareness of God's presence in the room and an assurance in our hearts that Jesus had touched Peggy not only to relieve her pain but to heal her cancer. Peggy was so relaxed that she excused herself, climbed into bed, and fell fast asleep.

Within a couple of days, the grapefruit-sized lump in Peggy's stomach had completely disappeared. When she told her husband what had happened, he insisted that she return to the local hospital for further x-rays. The doctors there could find no sign of the mass that had been clearly demonstrable on x-ray and physical examination a few weeks earlier, and they decided to send Peggy to the tumor clinic in Pasadena for further tests. When these results too were negative, Peggy's surgeon in Pasadena insisted on an exploratory operation to locate the cancer that, he felt certain, was still present. Peggy agreed to satisfy the doctor and surgery was performed.

On the way to the operating room, Peggy told her doctor, "You're going to be surprised." "Surprised" was an understatement! Although he practically took Peggy's insides out searching for the cancer, the surgeon could find only a few adhesions from previous surgery. When Peggy went to his office for her postoperative examination a few weeks later, he told her he just could not understand it. Peggy said, "Doctor, I could tell you what happened, but you probably wouldn't believe me." His reply was, "Try me and see!" With that, Peggy proceeded to give her testimony to this Jewish surgeon. When she had finished, he said, "Some things that happen can't be explained medically. I feel that your healing has been by divine intervention and is a miracle of God!"

A few weeks later I received another urgent phone call from Gwen. "Ruth, come to Peggy's quickly! She's dying!" When I arrived at Peggy's home a few minutes later, Gwen and Barbara were already there. I rushed into the bedroom to find Peggy in the throes of a severe asthmatic attack, propped up on pillows and gasping for breath. The three of us began to pray fervently, and in a short while the gasping stopped. Satan whispered in my ear, "Now you've done it! She's dead. You should have called an ambulance right away instead of wasting time with this ridiculous praying."

Gwen and Barbara looked as frightened as I was. I was just trying to summon the faith to ask Jesus to restore Peggy to life when Gwen put her ear down on Peggy's chest and exclaimed, "Her heart is beating!" After all of us had listened to the strong, regular heartbeat, we began to relax and to praise God for healing Peggy miraculously a second time.

I wish I could report that everyone for whom we pray receives healing—but this would not be true. Although I can't explain the cases in which the course of a fatal illness was not changed by "effectual fervent prayer" (James 5: 16), I do know that when this happens we are not to lose faith and stop believing God for future miracles. As I have tried to commit to the Lord things I don't understand, He often—though not always—gives me some insight into His purposes for allowing them. I do know that God's mercy is far greater than we can ever begin to comprehend, and that He has much more for us than we have ever claimed. Jesus paid a great price to give us the privilege of becoming His joint heirs, and He wants us to receive our full inheritance.

6

The Bubble Bursts

Bob speaking:

For about two years after our encounter with Christ, we rode the crest of the wave, and everything seemed to go our way. Then one memorable day a member of our church approached me about going into the restaurant business with him. The idea sounded tremendous, and I could visualize all the money we could make for the Lord. Ruth and I discussed the pros and cons of making such a venture and prayed about it together. We didn't have the capital needed but did have two pieces of property, both of which would have to be mortgaged if we were to go into business. In our prayers we asked God to block the deal if it was not His will for us to be involved in this business.

The deal was not blocked, and in just a few weeks we had leased the restaurant and felt we were on our way to financial success. Instead, we were on the brink of financial disaster. Within four months the restaurant was closed, after we had found that we were losing money at the rate of $500 a week.

The business failure was just the beginning of our financial problems. The construction firm by which I had been employed for five years—first as an electrician, then as foreman, and then as superintendent—also fell on hard times and had to lay off several employees. I was one of them—and for several months I was unable to find another job. Now, in addition to the debts that had accumulated as a result of our business failure, our domestic bills began to pile up. Some of our friends suggested that I file bankruptcy papers; but my feeling was that I had gotten myself into this situation and, by the grace of God, I would come through it and pay off all my debts.

Our faith in God's goodness and love was being put to the test—and it was tested still further when our daughter contracted lobar pneumonia and had to enter the hospital. This third blow was the one God used to show us that He can take a seemingly catastrophic situation and turn it into a testimony to His glory.

When our daughter was ready to be released, the hospital called and asked us to make arrangements for paying the bill when we came to pick her up. We had no money and limited hospital insurance which did not cover much of the bill. Before we went to the hospital business office, God had been speaking to the heart of our friend Gwen concerning our need. Gwen called Doris, a Lutheran friend from our prayer group, and the Lord impressed upon the two of them that we didn't have the money to pay the hospital bill. They shared this concern with others from the group, many of whom offered money to help meet this need. While Ruth and I were talking to the woman in the business office and telling her that we didn't know how the full bill would be paid—although we believed that God would take care of it somehow—Doris came in, unbeknown to us, and paid the balance. (As Doris was driving to the hospital she kept thinking, "Won't you feel stupid if the McKees have hospitalization insurance to cover the entire bill.") When we all had seen what God had done, tears of gratitude welled up in our eyes including those of the woman working in the office. This incident was responsible for leading several women from Doris' Lutheran church to seek and receive the Baptism in the Holy Spirit.

This was not the only time God intervened supernaturally on our behalf. During this period of financial distress, one of our bank notes was three months overdue, but the bank had not sent me a notice. When I phoned to check on our account, Ruth had many anxieties about what the loan officer would say. Suddenly the Scripture came to her, ". . . Whoever puts his trust in Him shall not be ashamed." [Romans 10:11 BERKELEY BIBLE] For a considerable time, the man to whom I was talking was unable to find our account. Then he came back to the

51

phone in great excitement and asked me to come to the bank on the following day.

At the bank, the loan officer began to apologize to me for the fact that the bank's business machinery had made a mistake in our account and that, for some unexplainable reason, our next payment was not due until June of 1970. (This happened in 1965.) I told him honestly that we did not have money at the present time to make a payment, and that I believed God had done this for us. Tears came to his eyes as I shared my faith with him—and from that time on the people at that bank greeted us as if we had a million dollars on deposit whenever we walked in. We felt that we had more than that, because we were backed by the Father, Son, and Holy Spirit. If our trust is in Him, truly we will *not* be put to shame!

One practical lesson we learned during this time of financial pressures was that keeping in contact with our creditors, even though we couldn't pay a cent on their bills, made them realize that we were sincere. Most of those to whom we explained our situation were willing to work with us. There are many times when we would like to hide from circumstances and not admit to ourselves—much less to anyone else— how bad things really are; but God wants us to face up to our problems and then to go forward in the faith that, with His help, they can be solved.

Although we could not understand at the time what was taking place or why, the Lord was preparing us for a future faith ministry as He proved Himself to us again and again. One Friday night, right after the restaurant had failed and I had lost my job, we attended a home prayer meeting in San Dimas. We told no one about our great financial need, but the cry of our hearts was, "Help, Jesus!" As we were leaving the home, the hostess handed Ruth an envelope, saying that it was from someone who wanted to remain anonymous. As we were driving back home, Ruth opened the envelope and found that it contained a cashier's check for $500! We were overwhelmed at this fresh evidence of God's faithfulness and concern.

"Why, God?"

Ruth speaking:

Even though we were seeing God meet our most pressing needs, we had periods of great discouragement. We were really questioning God as to why all this had come upon us, and we found ourselves losing the joy we had first known and doubting that we would ever find it again. The first two years of our walk in the Spirit had been relatively free of problems, but now our faith was really being tested. We recalled a comment that someone had made about us soon after we had received the baptism in the Holy Spirit. This woman, who was not in sympathy with the Pentecostal experience, said, "Who couldn't be happy with a nice new home and things going well? Let the problems and testings come into their lives, and then see what will happen to their 'experiences'!"

These words began to haunt me. As Bob remained out of work and our debts continued to mount, I began to wonder if God loved us so much after all. Satan kept whispering in my ear, "If this God you've been telling everyone about is so good, why is He letting you down? What will you tell the people now?" At times, he had me almost believing that God had actually cast us away from His presence.

Friends had quoted to us the verse from Paul's first letter to the Corinthians: "No temptation except what all people experience has laid hold of you, and God is faithful, who will not permit you to be tempted beyond your ability but will, at the time of temptation, provide a way out, so that you will be able to stand it." [I Corinthians 10:13 BERKELEY BIBLE] I knew that Scripture, but I felt the Lord was about to overdo it and I told Him so.

For a few months after our bubble burst, we felt a desire to withdraw from involvement in Christian activities; but we soon found that we needed the fellowship and prayers, as well as the counsel, of other members of Christ's Body. From the time we had opened our home for prayer meetings, we had felt responsible to God for the well-being of those who came. When the Lord allows you to have a responsibility like this, there is a temptation to feel that you must maintain an "image." Since people are coming to you constantly for help, you begin to think that you cannot mention your own needs. We felt that we had to look and act like victorious Christians, even when we desperately needed ministry ourselves. What a subtle trick of the enemy this is! All Christians, and especially those in positions of leadership, need the prayers of others. It is only when we humble ourselves and acknowledge our needs to our fellow Christians that we receive help.

During one of our periods of deepest discouragement, we went to a meeting in Corona, where Dr. Robert Frost was speaking. When the invitation was given for those who wished ministry to come forward, we were among those who did. Dr. Frost knew nothing of our troubles, and when he came to pray for us there was no time for conversation with him. Laying one hand on Bob's head and the other on mine, he began to pray. Almost immediately the prayer became prophecy, the essence of which was that God loved us and that the trials we were suffering were being allowed so that we might help others in *their* time of need, and that people would know God had been with us! My heart leaped in faith again. Oh, the goodness of our Lord to encourage us at times like these!

God sent us another message of encouragement through Gwen. She stopped by to see us one Saturday night, and told us that she had been feeling a burden to pray for us. Then Gwen shared a vision the Lord had given her while she was praying in the Spirit. She said she saw a stormy sea with a rock protruding out of the water. Bob and I were standing on the rock with a light lifted up in our hands. The winds blew and the storm raged, but we stood firm upon the rock until the winds quieted and a beautiful sky appeared—one of the most beautiful she had ever seen. Then she realized that out in the sea there were hundreds of people who were being drawn to the light we were holding, which was the Gospel. The Rock on which we were standing was Jesus. The storm and wind had tried to extinguish the light and drown Bob and me, but they had failed. Gwen's interpretation of this vision was that God had a work for us to do and that Satan was trying hard to defeat us. I remember having goose bumps (call it a witness of the Spirit, if you'd rather), and again I felt gratitude to God for ministering to us and encouraging us through His servants. From the day we had received the Baptism in the Holy Spirit, Bob and I had had a desire deep within us to reach out to others; and this vision reassured us that God was preparing us to be more effective witnesses for Him.

Three different times within ten days, we were given the same Scripture by three different persons:

"If you will humble yourselves under the mighty hand of God, in his good time he will lift you up.

Let him have all your worries and cares, for he is always thinking about you and watching everything that concerns you.

Be careful—watch out for attacks from

Satan, your great enemy. He prowls around like a hungry, roaring lion, looking for some victim to tear apart. Stand firm when he attacks. Trust the Lord; and remember that other Christians all around the world are going through these sufferings too.

After you have suffered a little while, our God, who is full of kindness through Christ, will give you his eternal glory. He personally will come and pick you up, and set you firmly in place, and make you stronger than ever."

[I Peter 5:6-10 THE LIVING BIBLE]

At times when my faith faltered, I wondered how long "a little while" would be. I was ready to be delivered and had been praying earnestly for deliverance, knowing that it was within the power of God to restore us to a position of financial security whenever He chose to do so. Before too long, however, I began to realize that He did not choose to do so immediately. Somewhere I had read the statement, "Many people are praying for deliverance when they should be asking to be developed." As these words were quickened to my heart by the Spirit, I began to accept the fact that God would take us *through* our present situation and not give us a quick way out, since we had much to learn.

7

The Jericho March

Bob speaking:

Although we had tremendous pressures, there remained a peace down deep inside. At times the Lord would allow me to be oblivious to the situation. I remember remarking at our prayer meeting one night, "It's ridiculous to feel this way with the circumstances as they are; but I have a real peace." During these times, I felt as though I were suspended above the problem.

Our greatest crisis came when we received the final notice from the mortgage company telling us that they were foreclosing on the house. If $1200 was not paid within two weeks, they would sell the house for the amount we owed on it. Since we had already attempted unsuccessfully to obtain money to make this payment, we had no idea where to turn. When we moved into the house a couple of years earlier, Ruth had made the comment that the house was God's and if we had to walk away from it we could. Now that we were faced with the possibility of having to walk away from "God's house" (which we had inevitably come to think

58

of as *our* house), we wondered if we really meant those words.

Remembering that Jesus had indicated that there is sometimes a need for prayers to be accompanied by fasting [Matthew 6:16], Ruth and I decided to begin a fast on Friday and to partake of nothing but water for three days. During this time we spent much time praying and reading the Scriptures, seeking an answer from God. Sunday morning we attended a church up in the San Bernardino mountains, where a good friend of ours was the pastor. We felt that maybe the Lord would speak to us through him. God did speak through him, but Ruth and I didn't share with each other the answer that each of us felt God was giving us.

The following evening we went to a meeting of the Full Gospel Business Men's Fellowship in Ontario, California. Through the main speaker at that meeting, God again gave us the same answer that He had on Sunday. When we got home from Ontario that night, Ruth and I finally shared what each of us felt God was saying to us. Both messages that were given had to do with Joshua's leading the Israelites into the Promised Land and taking the city of Jericho. The thing that most impressed us both was that God told Joshua to have the Israelites march around the city seven times on the seventh day (Joshua 6:4). We felt that God was saying to us, "March around this house seven times and claim it in My name!"

It was about 11 p.m. by now, and we imagined the neighbors would be in for the night. Looking around, we saw that all the houses were dark. If this was all God wanted us to do, we thought, it would be easy—but we didn't know what "old Smutty-face", the devil, had up his sleeve. We began our march from the front door, saying, "In the name of Jesus Christ we claim this house!" Our neighbors to the south were sitting around their swimming pool with the lights off. As we passed close to them, claiming our house for Jesus, someone called out "Tennis, anyone?" Our faith faltered, but we continued across the back yard (as the dog across the alley began to bark at us) and around to the north side of our home. We marched right by the Episcopal dean's bedroom window saying, "In the name of Jesus Christ we claim this house!" When we neared the completion of our first circuit, we saw that people were leaving the house across the street. Instead of going immediately to their car, they stood around and chatted for awhile in the front yard. As we came around to *our* front yard, speaking forth in a loud voice, "In the name of Jesus we claim this house," they gave us a startled look.

Feeling more than a little foolish, we continued to walk around the house, claiming it in the name of Jesus. About the third time around our faith began building up—and by the time we had gone around seven times it was so strong that we could have continued marching around the house day and night, with the whole world watching us! We felt the victory was ours. We didn't know how God was going to take care of the matter, but we had done what we felt led of the Lord to do. Our good friend J. A. Dennis from Austin, Texas, once said that we play a checker game with God: He makes a move and then we should make a move. Our move was made. Now it was up to Him.

"Don't Worry?"

Ruth speaking:

After Bob and I had marched our seven times around the house, the waiting began. This seems to be the place where many Christians panic. As the deadline for foreclosure of the mortgage got closer and closer, I began to wonder if God would really honor our faith in claiming the home. We came into the final two weeks and I was sitting on the couch looking out the patio door toward the San Bernardino Mountains. My heart was crying, "Help, Lord!" Seeing J. B. Phillips' translation of the New Testament lying close by (after our encounter with Jesus as Savior and then as Baptizer in the Holy Spirit, we had Bibles all over the house!), I picked it up and opened it at random. I found myself in the fourth chapter of Philippians and began reading at the fourth verse:

"Delight yourselves in God; yes, find your joy in him at all times." God was reminding me that my joy was in *Him*, not in the circumstances surrounding us.

"Have a reputation for gentleness, and never

61

forget the nearness of your Lord." This reminded me that I wasn't always gentle—and when I read the part about never forgetting the nearness of the Lord I began to weep because I had not acted in faith upon His promise that He would *never* leave us.

"Don't worry over anything whatever; tell God every detail of your needs in earnest and *thankful* prayer, and the peace of God, which transcends human understanding, will keep constant guard over your hearts and minds as they rest in Christ Jesus." For the first time, I saw "Don't worry" as a *command!* I had told God every detail of our need and I surely was in earnest; but I hadn't been very thankful. I didn't fully understand the power of praise at this time, but right then and there I began to give thanks to the Lord for all that He had done; for all that He is. Then I went on to read the next paragraph:

"Here is a last piece of advice. If you believe in goodness and if you value the approval of God, fix your minds on whatever is true and honorable and just and pure and lovely and praiseworthy. Model your conduct on what you have learned from me, on what I have told you and shown you, and you will find that the God of peace will be with you."

I found that I could discipline my mind to think on the above things which helped to keep the channel of my mind open to God and increased my faith to believe. Unfortunately we don't always continue to put into practice what God teaches us at each particular time.

I used these verses to ward off the darts Satan kept shooting at me. Whenever he would raise the question, "But what if . . . ?" I would immediately reject this line of thought and cling to the promise that God would take care of the situation concerning our house if I took Him at His Word and didn't give way to the sin of worry. In this way I found peace.

I was able to apply this and have a peace that we would not lose our home. We continually learn and grow. Had I appropriated this more later on in our Christian walk it would have eliminated some struggles. Many times we will receive instruction from the Lord and use it for that particular purpose and then not appropriate it later on. Our faith grows as we act upon God's promises. Some of us have to go to school longer than others!

"Yes, Don't Worry!"

Bob speaking:

While the Lord was showing Ruth how to fight off the fiery darts of Satan, He was teaching me also. I too had been saying, "But, Lord, what if something is not provided? What if we can't pay the light bill? What if we don't have food? What if we lose the house? What if, what if . . . ?" The answer I was getting from the Lord was, "I have been providing. The light bill has been paid. You do have food and you have not lost the house. *Thank Me* for what you have now and don't be concerned about what might happen in the future." How many Christians, like Ruth and me, torment themselves needlessly by *supposing!* Supposing this, or supposing that were to take place? Someone said that 90 percent of the bridges we worry about crossing never have to be crossed. If we could only learn to trust God in *all* things, how much easier this walk of faith would be!

On the Sunday before the deadline for our mortgage payment, Ruth went to church alone. (For some reason I don't recall, I couldn't make it that morning.) As she was on her way to the car after church, one of the ushers—an officer at a local bank—called to her, "Hi, Ruth! How are you and Bob doing?" She shared with him briefly about our situation. "Have Bob call me when you get home," Joe told her as she left him. Ruth relayed that message to me, and I called Joe immediately. He asked us to come to see him on Wednesday—a day or two before the deadline!

When we got to Joe's office, we gave him a more detailed account of our plight and how we had gotten into it. He asked us how much we needed to save the house; then without telling us the things we had done wrong or giving us a lecture on how to handle money, he wrote out a check for $1200 on his personal account. Joe had been asking God to let him help someone, and he told us, "I don't always know when God speaks to me to help others; but I know He wants me to help you now!"

As we paid the required amount to the mortgage company, we really praised God for His faithfulness—and for Joe! The house was ours until we sold it when we moved to St. Louis five years later. (We repaid Joe from the sale of the house along with interest.) Praise the Lord! God is able if we will only put our trust in Him and not doubt the promises he has given us in His word.

"Some Lessons We Learned"

Doubtless many readers have been wanting to ask, "If you prayed about going into the restaurant business, why would God allow you to go into the venture with such disastrous results?" I have no doubt that God heard our prayer and that He allowed us the freedom of desire in order to teach us some much-needed lessons—not just lessons in trusting Him, but lessons in exercising the common sense that He has given us. God never expects us to stop using our common sense. Someone once said that some Christians are so heavenly minded that they are of no earthly use—and there is an uncomfortable amount of truth in this accusation. Many Christians (like I did), sometimes throw common sense to the wind in making important decisions.

Our avowed purpose for going into business was to make money for God's work. This reason was valid, if our hearts and motives were pure. (I am not so sure mine were.) We came to realize, however, that God is not concerned about our making money for Him, for He owns the cattle on a thousand hills. [Psalm 50:10] He is concerned about our growing into the full stature of His son, Jesus Christ. [Ephesians 4:13]

Another thing we began to realize was the need to seek the counsel and advice of others more mature in the faith than we. Jesus said, "Where two or three are gathered together in my name, there am I in the midst of them." [Matthew 18:20] When we have an important decision to make, we should seek out those who are mature in the faith and whose judgment we respect, and ask them to pray with us that God's desire may be fulfilled. Then we should ask the Lord to confirm our decision from His written word. Many times we pray to know God's will and fail to realize that we can find His will in the Holy Scriptures. We had not done this before going into the business.

Another important lesson we learned was that Paul's admonition not to be unequally yoked with unbelievers [II Corinthians 6:14] applies to business relationships as well as to marriage. Light and darkness do not mix in a business any more than in a home. Although the man I had gone into partnership with was a member of our church, his ideas about God were very different from mine—and I soon learned that his ideas about operating a business were equally different. We were like a pair of mismatched horses pulling a wagon—never pulling together, but always heading in different directions; in other words, we were unequally yoked. Unless Jesus is the common denominator between partners—the basis for all their desires and decisions—there will be constant confusion and frustration in any relationship.

Another thing the Lord showed me was the foolishness of becoming involved in a business I knew nothing about and would not be able to take an active part in. Although my partner had managed restaurants previously, he had not told me how much money would be required to support a restaurant for the first six to twelve months, and I had not bothered to find out for myself. Our arrangement was that I would provide the capital and continue to work at my construction job, and he would operate the business. I had little time to check on the business—and if I had had the time, I probably would not have known what to check on!

Even though we got ourselves into financial straits by our own foolishness, God still used this stituation for our good. Through this experience He made us realize total (or near-total) dependence on Him. We were taught to be good stewards of the material gifts God gives us. Before the restaurant failure, we were habitual credit-card users, and we often found ourselves at the end of a month with more bills than money. God began showing us that He did not want us to be encumbered with debts, but to be free and flexible to move with Him. Immediately we tore up all of our credit cards. The Scripture He kept impressing on our minds—and it has been a part of our life ever since—is, "Owe no man any thing, but to love one another." [Romans 13:8]

It would seem that we paid a high price for these lessons that the Lord wanted us to learn; but actually their value to us is greater than all the money in the world. Much of what we had accumulated financially in nineteen years of marriage was lost; but spiritually we were richer than we had ever been before. The Lord had prepared us for the next step with Him.

8

Called Out

Bob speaking:

From the very beginning of my new life in Christ I had felt a desire to serve the Lord full time—an ambition that seemed impossible of fulfillment for a layman with a limited educational background. What frustration was in my heart! I kept crying out, "Lord, I am willing to be used, and you know how miserable I am in this construction work." (I was now employed again with another electrical company.)

I have since learned that many persons who have received Christ and have been baptized in the Holy Spirit have the same reaction: they desire to devote their entire time to serving God but do not know how to go about it. This is a very crucial period for a Spirit-filled believer— a time when he should really seek the mind of Christ. Many newborn and newly baptized Christians, in their zeal to serve God, miss His purpose for their lives by "running ahead of the Spirit." As I see it from the Scripture and from experience, God is not so greatly concerned about time as we are. To Him a day is as a thousand years, and a thousand years as a day. [II Peter 3:8] God wants us to be prepared before He calls us out into whatever work He has for us. Moses had 40 years of preparation for leading the children of Israel out of Egypt, and the apostle Paul waited on Jesus for three years before being called out. God wants us to be prepared when He calls us out, and He wants us to know without a doubt that we have been called to a fulltime ministry. He will teach us if we are willing, whether we are clergymen or laymen— and when He knows we are ready, He will lead us into the path He has prepared for us.

To those readers who might be in this period of waiting, I suggest that you not do anything hasty. Get into a good Bible study group taught by one of God's anointed teachers. Find a vibrant, Spirit-filled prayer group in which the members have a real love and concern for one another. If possible, be a part of a church that has a vision of what God is doing today. Then wait on the Lord's direction.

Even after I found work again, the period of waiting was a very trying one for me. The job in which I was employed during my last eight months in construction work was probably the most undesirable I had ever had, and I had to do a lot of praying to get through each day. I was working in a tunnel that was to bring water down from northern California to the southern part of the state. The tunnel was to be three and a half miles long, and when I came on the job it was about half done. Working underground was a new experience for me, and I found the dark, wet, smelly tunnel very depressing and somewhat frightening. We were working with high voltage and had to wear rubber pants, coats and boots, and a fiber hard hat. To top it all, the language of the workers who did the drilling was obnoxious. It sounded like me in the years before my conversion! If there was hell on earth, I felt I had found it.

I had been working on this job about two months when I had an experience that would have made a Christian of me if I hadn't already been one! About one-fourth mile from the main entrance, the tunnel divided into two forks. As the tunnel was being bored, a single track was laid from the entrance to the fork; then the track also forked. Two locomotives went back and forth over this track, hauling out the dirt and rocks from each heading and carrying workers to and from the places they were needed.

One day, as our crew was being taken into the tunnel to do some work, we noticed a red light indicating that a train was coming from the opposite direction. We waited before going in, as we were supposed to do, but there was no sign of the oncoming train. After waiting a few minutes, my foreman decided that the light had been left on by mistake and ordered our locomotive to proceed. As we came closer to the fork, we heard the rumble of the other train approaching on the same track. There was no siding for us to switch onto, and it was too late to signal the other train to stop.

I was on a flatcar with another worker named Charley, and the only thing I knew to do was kneel, pray, and wait. I was afraid that if I jumped off, the impact of the crash might cause a car to slam into me. The other locomotive was pushing nine cars full of dirt and rock. As it hit us, Charley was knocked off balance and started to fall under the wheels. I reached out and caught his hand; my knees seemed to be fused to the flatcar, and I was able to pull him to safety. Up to this point Charley had never testified to his faith in Christ—but this experience brought a testimony out of him in a hurry! He knew, as I did, that God's hand had held me on that car and kept both of us from going under the wheels.

While I was still working on the tunnel job, I was invited to go on a ministry trip to the Midwest with Ray Bringham, president of the Inter-Church Renewal Ministry. Over the past two years I had accompanied him several times on week-end and evening preaching missions, and I was tremendously excited and grateful when he asked me to go on this extended trip. We would be gone for two weeks and would hold meetings in Missouri, Illinois, and Indiana. We would be sharing about the renewal of the Holy Spirit in the churches today.

When I told Ruth about the invitation, I was disappointed that she didn't seem to share my enthusiasm. We had not been separated often during our years of marriage, and up until now we had always ministered together. She was willing for me to go, however, and said that as this was what God wanted it was what *she* wanted. I began to make preparations and soon was off on my first ministry trip.

In Saint Louis, Ray and I attended a dinner meeting which the local minister of the Inter-Church Renewal Ministry had arranged for the clergy. After the meeting, I noticed that one man started to leave and then came back. This happened several times before I finally went to him and began a conversation. I soon learned that he was a defeated minister who wanted to serve God but didn't have the power needed to do the job. With tears, he told me he was quitting the ministry and going into the insurance business. I suggested that he confess to God any areas of his life in which he needed forgiveness. After he had done this and had asked God to forgive him, we asked Jesus to baptize him in the Holy Spirit. What a change came over this minister as he was clothed with God's power— and how thrilled I was to be used as God's instrument in this way!

That trip to the Midwest was the start of a traveling ministry that has taken me into many states. Ray invited me to accompany him on several trips to Scottsdale, Arizona, for ministry among the Episcopalians. The Lord had been using me especially to pray with people to receive the Baptism in the Holy Spirit. With each trip, I could feel the Lord calling me into full-time work. On one of the trips Ray confirmed this impression when he said casually, "Bob, I believe God has called you out to a full-time ministry." My heart leaped at this confirmation of the call I had been feeling. The circumstances of my life at that time seemed to offer further confirmation: the tunnel job—to my great relief—had terminated and I was temporarily unemployed.

My first reaction to Ray's remark was, "OK, Lord, I'm ready to go as soon as You furnish a salary or an allowance." No salary or allowance was forthcoming, and I finally got the message God was giving me: "I have been preparing you all these months and allowing you to go through tests and trials so that you would learn to depend on Me alone." This idea took a bit of getting used to, for Ruth and I had become pretty dependent upon that check I received at the end of every week's work; but it didn't take me long to decide that if God wanted it this way I was willing to give it a try.

When I told Ruth that I felt God was calling me into a full-time ministry and that He wanted it to be one of faith, her reaction was less enthusiastic than I had hoped it would be. She knew I had a real zeal for the work of the Lord, and she wanted to be sure this was really a call from God and not just my zealousness. Knowing that security is more important to a woman than to a man, I knew God would have to speak to Ruth's heart also. I believe it is almost impossible for a man to do the work God has called

74

him to do if his wife is not in agreement. "Can two walk together, except they be agreed?" [Amos 3:3]

One morning, as I was preparing to go into Ray's office for the day, Ruth was washing the breakfast dishes and just talking with Jesus. She said, "Lord, if you want Bob to go into a full-time work of faith with the Inter-Church Renewal Ministry, then surely You can take care of our needs." No sooner had she prayed this prayer than the doorbell rang. Standing at the door was one of our Christian friends, a widow, who said she felt led of God to bring us a gift. With those words, she handed Ruth a check for $100. This gift, and the timing of it, had a profound impact on Ruth as well as me. Imagine my excitement on returning home that evening when I found that more money had come in, making a total of $617 that the Lord had provided in one day! Thus God confirmed His call to me by showing us both that it was fully within His power and His will to take care of our needs.

Even though doors of ministry began to open up as Ruth and I agreed to trust God to provide for us, we found that making the transition to a life of faith was not easy. For one thing, I found it hard to accept money for my services for the Lord.

Even though my work in the ministry was often exhausting—physically as well as mentally and emotionally—I somehow couldn't think of it as being the kind of work for which I should accept payment. Another problem was Ruth's unhappiness at being left out of my traveling ministry.

I have one bit of advice for anyone who is thinking of embarking on a ministry of faith: you had better make sure God has called you into it, because the tests will follow. Many people are attracted by the excitement and glamour of traveling to different parts of the world and being associated with Christians whom they have long admired. Such a ministry does have many rewards; but there is a price to pay. I believe the Lord allows Satan to test and try us in order to find out if we really are sincere about wanting to serve God, and if we really trust Him to provide for our needs.

The area of finances seems to be a favorite battleground of the enemy. If he can get us to take our eyes off the Lord and look at our circumstances, he knows he has a victory. Many a man whom God has called to a faith ministry has taken secular employment to tide his family over a financial crisis ("just until things get better") and has found himself trapped by the security he finds in a steady job. There are times, perhaps, when God would have one of His ministers go into secular work for a short period; but more often, I believe, He wants us to trust Him.

For the first few months of my faith ministry, our income was adequate and fairly steady; then it began to dwindle. As it did, our faith dwindled proportionately, until we began asking the Lord if we had heard Him right. Like

Gideon, we put out a second fleece—just for confirmation—and asked the Lord to give us another sign that we were really in His will. That week we received in the mail a letter with no return address containing a cashier's check made out in the amount of $500 and a typed note saying, "Gratefully given in the name of the Father, Son, and Holy Spirit." All we could say was, "Thank you, Jesus. Forgive us for our unbelief."

Although our faith was greatly strengthened by this sign, our financial situation remained shaky for some time. At one point we didn't have money to pay the gas bill, and the company sent a man out to turn off the gas. When we told him what our situation was, he asked if we were all feeling well—explaining that the company allowed an extension of time if anyone in the house was sick. To his solicitous inquiries about the state of our health, we replied that we felt "just fine." "Don't you have even a headache or a runny nose?" he persisted. Resisting the temptation to invent a slight sniffle, we again replied that we all felt fine. Then I thought, "Lord, it's Your move now!"

At that point, the man said, "I'm not going to turn off your gas, because you are both too honest. They would really get after me in the office if they knew this, but I just can't do it. I'm going to give you a few more days." With this, he turned, walked back to his truck, and drove off. We just looked at each other and said, "Praise God!" The very next day we received a check that paid not only the gas bill but all our other creditors as well.

Our financial situation gradually improved as more and more opportunities came for me to travel to other cities for ministry. Each trip, however, meant another separation for Ruth and me. After five years of sharing a ministry together, Ruth was finding it difficult to adjust to my traveling and ministering without her.

9

Left Behind

Ruth speaking:

Before our encounter with Jesus, Bob and I had many differing interests. Since we had given our lives to the Lord, however, we had been united in serving Him. When Bob became a part of Inter-Church Renewal Ministry and began traveling, I felt left out. God had many things to teach me personally, and because I was a "slow learner", Satan had his way with me for a time. If you are having a time of trial, ask God what He wants to teach you. In every situation He has a lesson for us to learn, and it will be profitable for us. The very thing that seems to "undo" us will be the thing that God uses as a molding tool to shape us more into his image. Just as material has to be cut away in making a dress according to the designer's pattern, so does there have to be some cutting away of the "flesh" if God is going to make us conform to the perfect pattern He has provided for us: the image of His Son [Romans 8:29]. We are the ones who determine the length and severity of God's pruning and chastening. Many times we want to blame God for our own hang-ups.

In the present situation, my hang-up was resentment—and when I allowed this favorite tool of Satan to open the door, he began to work on me. The more Bob was away from home, the more resentful and unhappy I became. I kept asking the Lord why He had saved us and let us share so much together, if the end result was to be this kind of separation. Deep down, I was really accusing God of not playing fair with me!

Many times I was so upset that I would go into our bedroom and cry for an hour or more. Some tears bring relief and cleansing. Weeping which stems from self-pity, however, brings nothing but swollen eyes and a soggy pillow. Finally, I began to realize that the Lord wanted me to get up from the bed, stand on my spiritual feet, and counterattack the enemy. Then I began to search my heart and the Scripture and to ask God what He wanted to teach me in all of this.

One of the first Scriptures the Lord gave me was, "Wherein ye greatly rejoice, though now for a season, if need be, ye are in heaviness through manifold temptations." [I Peter 1:6] I was still in heaviness and a long way from rejoicing—but I began to feel that there would be an end to the period of testing if I would just get on with learning the lessons God wanted to teach me. God is very practical, and, if we will just ask Him and then listen to Him and obey His Words, He will show us how to cooperate with Him in learning the lesson that He has for us in a particular situation.

The first lesson, it seemed, was to submit willingly to my husband's authority. Many Christian women need to learn this lesson! "The head of every man is Christ; and the head of the woman is the man" [I Corinthians 11:3]; yet over and over the woman tries to usurp the authority that belongs to Christ and help the Lord get her husband straightened out. I believe very definitely that husbands and wives should talk and pray things out together; but after the wife has expressed her opinion, God wants her to let her husband have the final say—and then accept his decision with good grace. If the decision is wrong (and it sometimes is), a wife's nagging will only make it that much harder for her husband to hear the Lord speaking to him about correcting it.

The next lesson the Spirit taught me during this time was how to deal with resentment. Satan continued to remind me how much God was using and blessing Bob and how little He seemed to be using and blessing me. Now, however, instead of letting resentment build up in my mind, I began praying about the situation. When Bob was away on a trip and I found myself comparing the excitement of his life with the home routine of mine, I would begin to pray for him, asking God to have His hand upon him and to fulfill His divine purpose in him. What a breakthrough this was for me! Getting my mind off myself and onto praying for another released me.

I found that if I let negative thoughts and attitudes build up in my mind, they soon became amplified until they colored my whole outlook on life. I asked Jesus to help me discern the thoughts I had and even my dreams at night. Satan had been tormenting me through dreams so I began to check all conscious and subconscious mental activity out with the Lord to see where it originated.

Another thing the Lord was teaching me during this time was humility—and He knows just how to do it! Satan loves to puff us up, and if the Lord pulls the rug out from under our feet, so to speak, it is for our own spiritual well-being —to remind us that we must always give God the glory.

During these lessons, the Lord would send me messages of encouragement just at the right moment—maybe in a magazine article or through the words of a friend. Many times I was ministered to and blessed by other Christians who had been through situations far more difficult than mine. By sharing their experiences with me, they brought me hope.

I feel that many people go astray during difficult times because they begin to reach out for help from sources outside those which God has provided: His Word, His Body of believers, and His Holy Spirit, who will enable us to keep our eyes and hearts on Jesus and to fight off the attacks of the enemy. Praying in the Spirit is a tremendous weapon available to Spirit-filled Christians but often neglected by them. Bob and I had led many to the Baptism in the Holy Spirit and had encouraged these newly baptized Christians to use their prayer language regularly; yet I had been neglecting this gift myself. Now I began praying in tongues every morning for a period of 30 minutes, knowing that the Spirit Himself was praying through me for my particular need [Romans 8:26]. The Lord was teaching me to start practicing what I had preached!

"Free at Last!"

Even though I was becoming aware of what God was teaching me, my progress wasn't steadily upward. There were times when Bob would return home from a trip full of joy and enthusiasm, and I would dampen his spirits in a hurry! The devil really fights when God is on the move and doing a work in your life. He is most active when God has a victory right around the corner for you. Now he started me thinking, "Perhaps God doesn't love me any more. Maybe He is playing favorites." The devil fanned that thought until he was once again having a field day with me!

One day Bob returned home from a trip to find me all out of sorts again. In desperation, he called our good friend, Florence Brubaker, and said he was bringing me over for prayer. I didn't want to go and sulked all the way to Florence's house. When we got there, Bob briefly explained the situation to her and then the two of them began to pray. In the past, I had occasionally teased Florence about her "binding and loosing" prayer [Matthew 18:18], but now I could see that it really got results! After resisting the Spirit for a short while, I finally broke down and began to weep—and Florence and Bob began to rejoice! Something had happened inside me, and I knew I had been set free from this spirit of resentment that had been disrupting my life and Bob's for the past eight months. It was such a glorious feeling to be free!

From that day on I began to have a victory over my resentment of Bob's new work—and soon afterward, God began to open doors of opportunity for me to travel with Bob. Once again we found ourselves united in the Spirit—more fully than ever before!

10

We Continue Our Schooling

Bob speaking:

The Lord continued to give us lessons in trust, especially in the area of finances. Once when our oldest son, Steve, was attending Oral Roberts University in Tulsa, Oklahoma, I planned to follow a speaking engagement in Arizona with a trip to a conference in Tulsa. I had my ticket to Arizona, plus $22 in cash—$20 of which I had saved for the purpose of taking Steve and his girl friend out to dinner. There was no money for the trip to Tulsa or for my return fare home. God had told us to trust Him, and this is what we were trying to do.

Just a few days before I was to leave for Arizona, a young Advent Christian minister named Ken Lawrence stopped by our house. He had just begun a faith ministry, and he and his family, three boys and a wife, were traveling in the Southwestern states ministering in a bread truck that had been converted into living quarters. As Ken was ministering to a group in our home the evening before I left for Arizona, the Lord spoke to my heart and told me to give him

85

$20. I said, "But Lord, I want to take Steve and his friend out to dinner, and I only have $22." He seemed to say, "I know all about that, but these people are just starting on a faith ministry and they need help and encouragement at this time." I was so overwhelmed by the Spirit that tears came into my eyes. As I put the money in a basket, I shared with the other people present what God seemed to be saying to me. A collection was taken—and when the Lawrences left our home that evening they were $75 richer.

The next morning I left for Arizona with $2 in my wallet and a song in my heart. In Phoenix, I was met by friends to whom I had ministered previously. They handed me an envelope, and in it I found $100! As I was faithful in obeying God's command to give what I had to His servant, He was faithful in giving back to me five fold. I went to Tulsa, treated the children to a good dinner, and was able to help with selling enough Christian books at the Inter-Church Renewal conference to pay my fare back to California.

Ruth speaking:

The Lord was also continuing my homework along with Bob's, teaching me to put my trust more and more in Him alone. During one of the many times when our finances were at a low ebb, Bob was returning from a trip and I was to meet him at the Los Angeles International Airport—55 miles from our home. I had half a tank of gas in the car, *two nickels* in my purse, and *no* credit cards! I began thinking, "If Bob isn't on that flight for some reason, I won't even be able to get out of the parking lot—much less back home!"

When emergencies like this had arisen in the past, I had sometimes borrowed from the tithe money that we set aside out of our income. Although I had always replaced the full amount, the Lord had been dealing with us about this practice. Once again I was strongly tempted to borrow a couple of dollars "just to be on the safe side, Lord"—but I felt the Spirit convicting me that this would show lack of faith and urging me to trust God. Resisting the temptation to take even *one* dollar from the tithe money, I drove on to the airport with my two nickels. On the way I began praising God and singing in the Spirit—I was filled with faith, knowing my God was equal to any situation.

Bob was on the flight, of course and had money to pay the parking lot attendant and fill up the gas tank. We went directly from the airport to a church meeting, where Bob took part in a panel discussion. After the meeting, one of the participating ministers shook hands with me and left in my palm *two $5 bills*—one for each nickel! God had increased my capital a hundredfold as I learned another lesson in trusting Him!

"Humble Yourselves, One to Another"

As I said earlier, God knows how to teach His children humility as well as trust. I received a postgraduate course in this department when a young Presbyterian minister, Bob Whitaker, came to Upland for some Inter-Church Renewal Ministry meetings. Ray Bringham asked if we would take care of him during the four or five days he was in our area. In the past, I had always enjoyed having ministers as guests in our home—but that was when money and food were plentiful. Now our pantry was almost bare, and there was no money to replenish it. I found myself hoping that he would decide to stay somewhere else!

When the phone call came saying that Bob would be at our home in about ten minutes, I became desperate. I had prayed until the last minute that the Lord would provide food for our guest or an honorable way out of our commitment to keep him in our home—but this prayer had been answered in the negative.

When our guest arrived, his genuine friendliness helped to put me more at ease. Sitting in the living room across from him, I finally swallowed my pride and laid it on the line: "I'm glad you're a minister and that you understand what it means to live by faith. We don't have much food in the house, and you'll have to 'pray in' your meals with us. You are most welcome to share what we have."

Once it was out, I felt a great sense of relief. I didn't have to pretend or cover up any longer. Almost immediately the doorbell rang, and there stood a friend with two bags of groceries! As we unpacked the bags together, Bob began asking me if I had any eggs—any this, any that. After receiving a negative reply to most of his questions, he left, telling me he would be back shortly.

When he returned an hour or so later, he was loaded with bags of groceries which he brought into the kitchen. This was almost too much for me, and I could hardly fight back the tears. Bob comforted me by saying that the Lord had been good to him, and that he really wanted to share his blessings with us. Realizing that the love of Jesus had prompted his generosity, I was able to accept his gift in the same spirit of love.

One of his purchases was a large bag of grapefruit. Up until then I had never been much of a grapefruit-eater—but these tasted delicious, and I have loved grapefruit ever since! To this day, we think of Bob Whitaker whenever we have grapefruit.

"His Eyes are on the Sparrows—Cats Too!"

The Lord used our son's pet cat, Summer, to teach us that no living creature is outside the scope of His love and care. As Bob and I came home from a meeting late one night, David ran up to us crying, "Summer is dying! Summer is dying!" We hurried with David to the rumpus room, where we kept the box containing Summer's newborn kittens. Summer was lying on the floor outside the box, with her back end badly flattened. Apparently she had been hit by a car. David told us he had found her earlier in the evening, lying in the front yard unable to walk. He had carried her into the house and placed her on the floor where we found her.

Although it seemed that the sensible thing to do would be to have Summer put to sleep, Bob and I agreed to pray for her, in response to David's earnest request. Gently laying hands on the cat, we asked Jesus to heal her. Then, although David was still upset, we persuaded him to go to bed—and Bob and I followed suit.

The next morning I got up early, figuring that Summer would probably be dead (you can see how great my faith was!) and wanting to get her body out of the house before David found it. I went into the rumpus room, dreading what I would see. To my amazement, Summer was in the box nursing her kittens—completely healed! What a testimony this miraculous healing was to all our children, and to Bob and me as well! It helped us to understand more that the God who sees every sparrow that falls to the ground [Matthew 10:29] is also concerned with pet cats.

"Las Vegas Revisited"

Bob speaking:

As we slowly and sometimes painfully learned our ABC's of trust, obedience, and humility, the Lord led us into new areas of ministry in many cities and states. Although Ruth was traveling with me more and more, I still made frequent trips alone. One of these was to Las Vegas, where Ruth and I had spent a week-end before we became Christians. On that trip, I began shooting dice and winning. Ruth, being a much more conservative person than I, kept begging me to quit while I was ahead. I told her then that the next time I came to Las Vegas I was going to leave her at home.

Sure enough, I returned to Las Vegas without her—but instead of shooting dice in the Showboat Casino, I went to tell people about Jesus Christ and the Baptism in the Holy Spirit in a room above the casino. What a difference meeting the Lord Jesus Christ makes in a person's values and desires! This time the stakes were much higher and the winnings were for keeps!

11

We Are One in the Spirit

Bob speaking:

In the summer of 1968 a meeting with Father Francis MacNutt, a Roman Catholic priest from Saint Louis, marked the beginning of a totally new ministry for Ruth and me. Father MacNutt, a priest of the Dominican order, had just recently received the Baptism in the Holy Spirit when we heard him speak at an Inter-Church Renewal Ministry meeting in North Hollywood. Ruth and I were so much impressed with his message that we told him of our plans to be in Saint Louis (our home town) a few weeks later and asked if we might get in touch with him then. He cordially urged us to call him as soon as we arrived.

Our visit to Saint Louis later that summer "happened" to coincide with a ten-day workshop being held at the Academy of the Visitation (a convent and elementary and high school for girls). This workshop, attended by 150 nuns from all across the United States, was being held for the purpose of discussing aspects of church and community life. Father MacNutt was scheduled to speak on the final day of the workshop, and he invited us to attend that meeting with him. In our telephone conversation, he also gave us the name of a young Catholic woman, Maria Rossow, who was interested in the Pentecostal movement.

When we called Maria, she asked if we would come to the home of her parents to give our testimony. We were most happy to have the opportunity, and agreed to come on Thursday night—the night before we were scheduled to attend the workshop with Father MacNutt. Excitement welled up inside us at the prospect of sharing with two groups of Catholics in the space of two days. Up to this point Ruth and I had not ministered to many Catholics.

Thursday night was stormy, and tornado warnings had been issued. As we were on our way to the Rossow's house, Ruth commented, "People would really have to be spiritually hungry to come out in weather like this." At the Rossow's, however, the atmosphere was one of peace and love, and we felt at ease immediately. As we shared our testimony with Maria's family and a few of their friends, we were very conscious of the presence of the Lord.

After we had spoken and answered some questions, we offered to pray with anyone who wanted to receive the baptism in the Holy Spirit. Nearly all those present expressed a desire for this experience. I prayed with Maria while Ruth prayed with Maria's sister, Sari. Both began to speak forth in a new language as

Jesus baptized them in the Holy Spirit. We then prayed with Hav Bauer, Sari's husband, and with Maria's parents, Carl and Betsy. They too received, and the room was filled to overflowing with love as we praised God together in this new dimension. That night was the beginning of a special friendship.

"The Holy Spirit Falls at Visitation Academy"

The following afternoon we met Father Mac-Nutt at Visitation Academy, where he spoke on "prayer in the church." At the end of his talk, he remarked that the Pentecostal movement in the Catholic Church was introducing new ways of worshiping God. "If you want to know more about this," he said, "come back tonight at 7. Bob and Ruth McKee from California will be sharing their testimonies." The workshop ended, and we were invited to have dinner with the sisters. It was a privilege for us to be there and to share their gracious hospitality and their love.

Some 80 to 100 of the sisters attending the workshop returned for the evening meeting to hear about the Pentecostal movement. Father MacNutt introduced Ruth and me, and after we had given our testimonies, our new friends, the Bauers and Maria, shared what had happened to them the night before. After an hour or so, Father MacNutt announced that there would be a short break for refreshments, and that any who desired to receive the baptism in the Holy Spirit could remain for prayer afterward.

As Ruth and I, with Father MacNutt, were preparing to have a sip of punch, two nuns came up and asked if they could have prayer immediately. Finding a quiet room, we talked to them and found that one was a Mother Superior from Baltimore. She shared a personal prayer request, which we offered together to the Lord. Opening my Bible I read from the book of Acts the accounts of individuals and groups in the early church as they received the Holy Spirit. After a short time of instruction, both the sisters knelt for prayer. As Father MacNutt and I laid hands on them and prayed, they began singing in a beautiful new language. Feeling that they wanted to be alone at a time like this, we went back to the others.

To our amazement, about 80 sisters remained for prayer after the refreshment break was over. I had prayed with many people to receive the Baptism in the Holy Spirit before—but I must admit that the prospect of praying for 80 nuns was a bit overwhelming! Wanting to make sure they understood what I meant, I said, "All those who want ministry, to receive the Baptism in the Holy Spirit, put your hands together in an attitude of prayer." As I looked out over the group, almost all of them had their hands together. They also had head coverings on, and looked so starchy that I wasn't sure where to lay my hands as I prayed with them. I sent up an SOS: "Lord, what do I do now?" It seemed as if God spoke to me in His still, small voice saying, "Pray with them the same way you would pray for anyone else." I instructed the sisters on how to receive, and then those of us who had shared with them began praying for them individually. They were very quiet as they received their prayer language, and the presence of the Holy Spirit was real and sweet.

We became so involved in praying for the larger group of nuns that we forgot about the two sisters we had left in the other room. When we went back to them in about an hour, they were still kneeling on the concrete floor praising God in their new language.

"A Second Visit to Visitation Academy"

Among the nuns baptized in the Holy Spirit that night were five from the Visitation Academy Convent. We encouraged these to continue to meet together for fellowship in the Spirit. Father MacNutt met with them—and when Ruth and I came back to St. Louis in October we found that the group had grown from 6 to 60—a tenfold increase in two months! It now included priests, Catholic laymen, nuns and Protestants.

Ruth and I met with the group and again gave our testimonies. After about an hour of sharing, a refreshment break was announced.*

---

*We have noticed that the refreshment break seems to be characteristic of Catholic meetings. Besides allowing both the speakers and the listeners to quench their thirst and to have a brief time of fellowship, it also provides an opportunity for anyone who feels captured to make a getaway!

As at the previous meeting, two people came to Ruth and me before we had a sip of our punch and asked if we would pray with them to receive the Baptism in the Holy Spirit. Again we found a room where we could have privacy, instructed the two from the Scripture, and then prayed with them. Immediately they both began to praise and worship the Lord in a new language as Jesus baptized them in the Holy Spirit.

After a short time of worshiping together, we all started back to the larger meeting—but when the door was opened we found a line of people waiting to come in! Inviting them all into the room, we again went through the Scriptures showing Jesus as Baptizer in the Holy Spirit. What hunger was in their hearts! After giving them instructions on receiving the Baptism, we began to minister to them individually. Ruth began at one end of the row and I at the other, as the Lord poured out His Spirit upon them.

After the time of prayer was finished, we again started to leave the room to have our refreshments. On opening the door, however, we found that *another* line had formed! Inviting this group in, we went through the same procedure with them, and again the Lord faithfully filled them with His Holy Spirit. Before the evening was over, 35 or more had received the Pentecostal experience. The presence of God was so powerful that the air seemed to be charged with electricity. Ruth and I never did get to our drink—but who wants punch when he can drink from the fountain of living waters!

After the third delegation had been baptized in the Holy Spirit, small groups began to form all over the building, the members of each group ministering to one another. While Ruth was praying with a young sister in one room, I was with a group in another part of the building praying for a young deacon. He shared with us how discouraged and frustrated he had become, and said he was thinking of giving up studying for the priesthood. As he poured out his heart to God and asked for more reality in his life, Jesus baptized him in the Spirit.

What a change came over him as the joy of the Lord poured into him! As his new language of praise and worship burst forth, I could see the change within him reflected on his face. "I feel like a 150-pound weight had been lifted from me!" he shouted, as he began hugging those around him. Then he ran out of the room to share the good news with others. When he came to the Mother Superior, he picked her up and danced in circles! Those watching the disciples on the day of Pentecost thought they had been drinking new wine [Acts 2:13]. If anyone who did not understand had been watching us on that night, I am sure they would have thought that the punch had been spiked!

About 12:30 a spontaneous desire arose among the Catholics to have a mass to celebrate what God had done that evening—the Mass of the Holy Spirit. The priest chosen to celebrate it had been baptized in the Holy Spirit just three weeks earlier, and his assistant had received just that night. After beginning with the liturgical order, the mass went into a spontaneous, Spirit-led time of worship and praise to the Lord. At "The Peace", which is an exchange of handshake and greeting in the new Catholic liturgy, everyone was hugging everyone else, and one sister was heard to say, "I imagine it was like this in the catacombs." The truth of the song given us by the Catholics—"We Are One in the Spirit"—certainly became evident that night!

"A Meeting with the Jesuits"

The next day Ray Bringham came in from California, and that night the three of us met with some of the Jesuits who were a part of the faculty at Saint Louis University who also wanted to hear about the Holy Spirit movement. Although Ray is an ordained Church of God (Anderson, Ind.) clergyman, he told us later that the presence of those men of learning almost gave him "faith failure." He added, "I sure would have liked to have someone back me up theologically—but I only had an ex-electrician and a housewife!"

After Ray had shared the Scriptures with them, Ruth and I gave our testimonies. Most of those present seemed to be open and genuinely interested. People can debate theology, but no one can challenge your experience with God. Many of the Jesuits came to us afterward and told us they knew *about* God but had not experienced Him as we had. We prayed with many that night, that they might find the reality they were seeking.

All of us were invited to return to Saint Louis University the next day to give our testimonies to a class which was studying the theology of the "God Is Dead" movement. Again we did not discuss doctrine or theology, but just shared Jesus and what He had done in our lives. When the class was over, one young deacon came up to us and said, "You all sound like the apostle Paul. You sound as if you have been with Jesus!" At a later meeting, he too found the reality we were talking about.

We were in St. Louis for about a week on this second visit, and every day was packed with ministry to Catholics in homes, convents, and wherever there was a hunger. Before we returned to California, some of the sisters told us they were praying for God to move us into the Saint Louis area to live. We thanked them for their prayers and told them we were willing to make the move if that was God's desire.

12

Meet Me in Saint Louis

Bob speaking:

After coming back to Saint Louis in November and December of 1968, my next visit was in May of 1969, with Rodney Lensch—a Lutheran minister. Rod and I had met at a ministers' meeting in Burbank, California in 1967. He had pastored a church in Thousand Oaks, California, but resigned that position to travel as a teacher and evangelist. We were now working together in the Inter-Church Renewal Ministry. Our present plans were to spend four days in Saint Louis between meetings in Colorado and a weekend conference in Michigan. On Tuesday we found out that the conference in Michigan was called off. As the ministry in Saint Louis began to unfold, we could see God's hand in this cancellation. In addition to sweet times of fellowship with our Catholic friends, we had planned—through a friend of Rod's who is a Lutheran minister—to hold an ecumenical, charismatic meeting at Concordia Seminary which is Missouri Synod Lutheran. Since Saint

Louis is the headquarters for this segment of Lutheranism, we felt this was a miracle of God!

There was a tremendous anointing on the meeting at Concordia that Monday night and the presence of the Holy Spirit must have been felt by everyone there. Hav Bauer, one of our Catholic friends, had a vision in which he saw the Lord Jesus come into the meeting and lift us up to the Father for his blessing. What a glorious night it was as Catholics and Protestants from many denominations came together in a Lutheran Seminary to worship Jesus Christ in the Holy Spirit! As we sang our songs of praise together, it was as though an angelic choir joined in. Many received Christ as their Savior before the night was over, and others were baptized in the Holy Spirit.

The Lord blessed me that night by arranging to have Ruth fly in from California in time for the meeting. Her presence there was a complete surprise to me—and almost as great a surprise to her; but that part of the story is hers to tell.

"All Things Are Possible"

Ruth speaking:

After Bob had left on the trip to the Midwest, I kept feeling that the Lord was going to send me to Saint Louis to meet Bob in time for the meeting at Concordia Seminary. Although such a trip for me seemed impossible from the financial standpoint, I was so sure the Holy Spirit would arrange it that I got my household chores all caught up, made arrangements for the care of our youngest child, and even made a plane reservation. Each time the impossibility of making the trip came to my mind, it would be overruled by the words, "All things are possible to him who believes." [Mark 9:23]

Bob called me on Sunday morning from Denver, and I thought, "This is it! He's going to ask me to meet him in Saint Louis. He probably has my plane fare." It was a disappointment to learn that he was calling just to check on the children and me. After hanging up I thought, "Well, there goes that"—but I didn't cancel my plane reservation. The idea that nothing was impossible if I would just continue to believe would not leave my mind.

That afternoon I took a walk, and when I returned to the house the phone was ringing. The call was from some of our Catholic friends in Saint Louis who had been praying about the meeting at Concordia and felt impressed to call me and see if I could possibly come. They wanted to pay my expenses. I replied, "I already have my reservation made, and I'll be there!" Our friends met my plane the next evening, and we arrived at Concordia just in time to surprise Bob before the meeting began. No one had told Bob I was coming.

This experience was a real faith-builder for me, who always wanted everything laid out in advance. God's ways are truly different from ours, and we miss much that He wants to do for us by not listening to that still, small voice and obeying it in faith—no matter how insurmountable the obstacles seem to be.

"Moving Time"

Bob speaking:

What excitement was in my heart when we returned to California! God had shown Rodney Lensch, Ruth, and me the potential harvest to be reaped in Saint Louis, and now I could think of nothing but the Midwest. The Lord was putting a hunger in my heart to move back to Saint Louis—but Ruth and I wanted to make sure that this desire was really of God. We had learned from past mistakes to "lean not unto [our] own understanding" [Proverbs 3:5] and not to trust our own inclinations.

We knew that if God wanted us to make this move, He would have to sell our house in Upland. We had had the house on the market for about three years (we felt we could not afford to be in it after the restaurant failure), but so far, none of our would-be buyers had been able to purchase it. As Ruth and I thought and prayed about the move, we decided to use the house as a "fleece" [Judges 6:36] by listing with a realtor for three more months. If it didn't sell within that time, we would take it off the market and continue to live in it. If it did sell, this would be our sign that the Lord wanted us to make the move.

The house was sold within two months—at the price we were asking. We felt that God had given us a green light for the move to Saint Louis—and once the decision was made, it seemed that He was working with us in every possible way.

Because it was just two months before the end of the school year, we wanted to postpone the move long enough to let our children finish the term. God allowed us to stay in the house and pay rent during those months.

In order to save the expenses, we decided to rent a U-Haul truck to move our belongings to Missouri. When I went down to the rental agency to reserve a truck, I found that someone had already made the necessary deposit for me.

Much as we longed to say a personal "good-bye" to each of the many friends we had made during our fourteen years in California, we knew that it would be impossible to do so. The Lord also provided the answer to this "soul's sincere desire," by putting it into the hearts of some of our friends to give us a farewell dinner. That night will be long remembered!

Over 100 of the friends who had become a part of our new life in Christ were present as a "This is Your Life" skit was unfolded. This was about the time of the first heart-transplant operations—and one of our Lutheran friends, Ron Fowler, found a news item about a patient named Bob McKee who had received such a transplant. Waving a newspaper which carried that headline, he came running into the dining room calling "Read all about it! Read all about it! Bob McKee gets a new heart! "How true this was—but my "new heart" was not put in by the hands of a surgeon. God had given it to me according to the promise made to His children through the prophet Ezekiel [36:26–27].

Rod Lensch and his wife Joyce, who were to follow us to Saint Louis, were also present at that farewell dinner. In the meeting which followed the skit, prophecies came forth that gave direction to them and encouragement to us— encouragement that we greatly needed later on. To climax the evening, a love offering was taken for Ruth and I in toy U-Haul trucks.

A few days later, all our worldly possessions had been packed into the rented truck and we were ready to leave California. With tears in our eyes and lumps in our throats, we said "goodbye" to the "Jericho home" God had allowed us to live in for seven years.

13

Eastward, Ho!

Bob speaking:

We started out on June 14, 1969, for Saint Louis early in the evening, after having dinner at the home of our dear friends, John and Florence Brubaker. Because the desert is so hot during the summer months, we wanted to travel across it at night. Ruth, Toni, and I were in the U-Haul truck, and our three boys—Steve, Danny, and David—followed us in Danny's VW. The company we rented the truck from had a slogan which said, "An Adventure in Moving." Our trip was not too adventurous. We drove all night the first night, wishing to cross the California and Arizona deserts in the cool of the night. Ruth drove for about an hour at 2 a.m., and that was exciting enough to wake me up; I had been trying to sleep for awhile. We lost the boys who had gone on ahead of us and were to meet us in Flagstaff, Arizona, but we finally got together again in the next town. We ran out of gas further along in New Mexico, and I had to hitch a ride to a gas station leaving Ruth and Toni in the truck back on Highway

66. The boys had gone on ahead of us again, so they were not behind to give help. After this we told them to follow behind in the event we needed them. The third night on the road we stopped in Tulsa, Oklahoma, and I managed to park the truck and trailer in the motel parking lot without too much difficulty. When we left Tulsa, we were on the final lap back into Missouri.

Although Ruth agreed with me that God was leading us back to Missouri, she was not happy about the change in location. She loved California and felt that nothing could equal the beauty of the mountains near our home in Upland. As we approached the Missouri state line after three days of traveling, I said to her, "Look how pretty the countryside is!" Her reply was, "I don't think it's pretty; in fact, nothing around here is pretty. Even the cows are ugly." Needless to say, I didn't comment on the scenery again!

After driving awhile in silence, I said, "Why don't we listen to the tape that was made at our farewell dinner?" Ruth switched on the tape player, and again we heard God speak to us through a manifestation of tongues and interpretation. How much more meaning it had this time! In essence the message was, "Don't look to the left or to the right. I have called you to a steady work. While others are on a holiday, I have called you to do my work." Both Ruth and I knew that God was saying, "I know all about your feelings, but I have chosen you for this job at this time." A quietness settled on both of us as we drove on into Saint Louis.

"Doing God a Favor?"

Ruth speaking:

Our trip to Missouri—part of it through the desert—was truly a "wilderness experience" for me. Like the Children of Israel under Moses, I was murmuring against God all the way—and about the time we passed Joplin, Missouri, on Highway 66 my heart really began to sink. Oh, I didn't *want* to move back to Saint Louis! I knew there would be severe trials and testings awaiting us there. For one thing, we had no place to live. For another, my mother, my sister and her husband, and numerous uncles and aunts lived in the suburbs—and how could I ever explain this walk of faith to them?

Shortly after Bob and I had received the Baptism in the Holy Spirit, I had written my sister to tell her about our experience. After reading my letter, she felt that she had to fly out to California to see what in the world we had gotten involved with! After spending a week with us she returned to Saint Louis and reassured my family that we still seemed like normal people, even though we said "Praise the Lord" all the time and held prayer meetings in our home. She also admitted that she had felt a peace in our home that had not been there on her first visit.

But now God's will had definitely crossed

mine in this Saint Louis move, and I was having trouble submitting to Him completely. Even though I had agreed to the move and had made the necessary preparations, my heart was not completely in it—and the closer we got to Saint Louis, the more unhappy I became. I finally cried out deep within, "Help, Jesus! Help!" And help me He did. Right then Bob had me turn on the tape player, and the words of the interpretation given at our farewell dinner in Upland brought me comfort and encouragement.

For a long time after we were settled in Saint Louis, I still became teary-eyed whenever I thought of California, and I felt that I had done God a big favor by moving back to Saint Louis. The Lord reminded me of the time when I had told Him I'd go anywhere He wanted us to go —but I told Him that I never thought He would send us back to Saint Louis! Africa, yes; Saint Louis, no! Of course, my murmurings only made things worse, and the Spirit began showing this to me and convicting me that I would have to submit wholeheartedly before I could regain the peace I had known before. Slowly, over a period of many months, I began to submit and to adjust to our move back to Saint Louis.

Why do we struggle so hard against the Lord? He always knows what is best for us and knows just where to place us for certain levels of our Christian walk in order to accomplish His purposes in us.

"Settling Down"

Bob speaking:

Our first need on returning to Saint Louis was to find a place to live. When we shared this need at a prayer meeting a couple of nights after our arrival, one of our Catholic friends spoke up and said that his mother was out of town for the summer and her home was vacant. "The house is just a few blocks from here," he added. "If you want to look at it, we can run over there now."

We found the house suitable in every respect. It was completely furnished and had a large double garage that would be perfect for storing our furniture. Furthermore, it was air-conditioned—and anyone who has spent a summer in Saint Louis knows what this would mean! I said, "Bill, it's too good to be true! Do you think your mother would be willing for us to use it?" He told me he would call her the next day.

On the phone, Bill's mother graciously agreed to let us move into her lovely home for a few weeks and to store our furniture in her garage. How we praised the Lord! We were able to get the truck back to the rental agency on time— and when we totaled up the costs of moving, we found that the love offering taken for us at the farewell dinner in California came within a few dollars of paying for the entire move!

Before Bill's mother returned from her vacation, we were able to rent a small three-bedroom house in the suburbs. We had just moved in when Joyce and Rodney Lensch and their three girls arrived from California. It was fortunate that our two oldest boys, Steve and Danny, had gone back to California a few days earlier—for the Lensches had not found a home and we were able to invite them to stay with us until a house became available for them three months later.

This experience in "communal living" was to be the first of many tests of our love for one another. We soon found that it is one thing to shake a person's hand or even give him a hug and say, "I love you"—but quite a different thing to live with that person (and his pregnant wife and three young children) 24 hours a day. Living that close is almost like marriage, and —as is the case of most marriages—the only One who can make it work is Jesus. By putting us together and allowing us to rub our rough edges against one another, He was making us fit building stones for the temple He is framing together [Ephesians 2:21].

As our families spent these three months together, we found God dealing with all of us in many areas. It was necessary for all of us to keep our eyes on Jesus and to keep the channels of communication open. The Lord began to show us that He wants to be our strength in all things and all circumstances, and wants us to bring our flesh into subjection to the Holy Spirit. The tendency of the flesh is to run away from problems; but God is developing in us something eternal—and this requires submission and obedience, which most of us can learn only through times of testing. We can rebel against God's schooling and find ourselves remaining spiritual babes and miserable; or we can face up to our problems, yield to the Holy Spirit, and learn what God wants to teach us. The sooner we learn our lesson, the shorter will be the period of chastening.

"The Pressure Cooker"

One of the things God wanted to show me was that I had a possessive attitude. I had been praying that God would send teachers to Saint Louis to continue the work that had been started here. When He answered my prayers by sending Rodney Lensch and his family to minister with us, He also revealed the fickleness of my desires. The Scripture says that "the heart is deceitful above all things." [Jeremiah 17:9] After Rod arrived, I was not too sure I wanted him around. As he began to teach those whom I had fathered in the Spirit and had grown to love very much, I found myself becoming upset at their attention to him. At times I resented his leadership, although I knew God had sent him to teach.

Pride and possessiveness are Satan's tools—and with them he was attempting to destroy not only my friendship with Rod but my relationship with a few other Christians in Saint Louis. The Lord began to show me that those toward whom I felt possessive were *His* sheep, and that He would decide what part each of us had in feeding them. The ministry was His, the people were His, and *I* was His—so that didn't leave me much to be possessive over.

Another lesson the Lord had for me to learn was that I was not a Jack-of-all-trades who could take care of all situations. The Body of Christ has many members, and each depends upon the others [I Corinthians 12:12-31]. God was showing me that one would plant, another would water, and He would give the increase [I Corinthians 3:6]. Also God was saying that the newest babe in Christ is an integral part in the Body. Oh, how hard it is to take suggestions or teaching from those younger in the Lord than yourself!

After having experienced each other in this type of pressure cooker, Rod and I found a real love that was not present before. If we Christians can't love and understand one another now, how can we live in eternity together? In his teaching on the Twenty-third Psalm, Bob Mumford gives the answer to this question. He tells of talking to the Lord and saying, "You must love me very much to let me live in Your house—and especially *forever!*" The answer he received from God was, "Mumford, by the time you get to My house I am going to change you so much that I will be able to live with you!"

As I examine myself and consider my spiritual growth toward our example, Jesus Christ, I wonder sometimes, "God, is it possible that such

114

a person as I could ever be fit to live in Your house?" Even as I ask the question I know the answer, because it is in God's Word. Paul knew it is possible, for he wrote the Philippians: "Being confident of this very thing, that he which hath begun a good work in you will perform it until the day of Jesus Christ." [Philippians 1:6]

The first couple of years in Saint Louis were difficult ones in many ways, and Ruth and I needed all the preparation and strengthening God had given us through our experiences in California. Shortly before we left California, I was given a prophecy that this move would be the greatest test of my faith thus far. So it proved to be!

14

The Saint Louis Blues

Bob speaking:

After being associated with the Inter-Church Renewal Ministry for four years, I had severed that tie in order to answer God's call to Saint Louis. I was not sure what God wanted of us in Missouri, but He had given me a burden to see Spirit-baptized Christians continue their growth toward maturity—for we had seen many who had not moved beyond the milk-feeding stage [I Corinthians 3:2]. My desire was somehow to be a part of a teaching center in the Midwest.

A few months after our move from California, a group of us men met together for prayer, asking the Lord for guidance and direction; He seemed to speak to six of us to meet again. As we six men came together in prayer, we felt that God was directing us to form a teaching ministry for those who desired to hear God's Word taught in the power of the Holy Spirit. We had found that many Christians were spiritually dead or dying because of lack of such nourishment in their own churches. We did not want to take the place of a church, but rather to support and complement the established churches in any way we could.

All six of us believed that God had brought us together, and we formed a board as a preliminary step to organizing a teaching ministry. A few months after the board was formed, three of the six members felt led to resign. I couldn't understand how they could have had a change of heart so quickly, and I began to question their motives and to question God. After the first separation, others followed, and there were misunderstandings and bad feelings among the brethren involved.

Since that time, I have learned that God sometimes puts a group of people together for a specific purpose and then allows a separation to come. In situations like this we have to release one another and pray that every person involved is doing what the Holy Spirit directs—no matter how strongly we may feel that some are not! (A few minutes of prayer are worth more than a thousand words of correction.) Many times we give credit to the devil for causing such a separation—when all the time it is God who is allowing the shake-up for our own good. One of the brothers who resigned wrote me a letter which expressed this idea very beautifully:

The Lord has placed within each of us a measure of light by which He guides, directs, and reveals His will for us. My progress in this light is dependent upon my death; no one else can die for me. Each of our paths is woven in a divine type of maze —sometimes crossing, sometimes moving together, sometimes moving away from each other—designed to culminate in the full bloom of the Body of Christ.

I wish I could say that I was able to respond in a completely Christlike manner to this shattering of our plans—but that would not be true. The next several months were very difficult, and many times I threatened the Lord by saying, "Get someone else to do this work. I am not cut out for this walk of faith." Everything seemed to be going wrong: finances again tightened; ministry invitations stopped coming in; and deep, deep discouragement set in. It seemed that we were boxed into a canyon with only sheer cliff ahead and all of hell's demons at our heels.

"More Lessons"

Ruth speaking:

God had still more schooling for us. We experienced many wounds in the household of the brethren—and these hurt so much more than those that come from unbelievers! I felt that the Lord had shut our mouths and we were not to defend or justify ourselves in any way—but oh, how I wanted to so many times! I was to learn that God is the One who will defend and justify us, and we are not to make any effort to do this for ourselves.

I must acknowledge that we also inflicted wounds on others, and that we made many mistakes in the months that followed the dissolution of the original teaching ministry board. I reached the place where I felt that I never wanted to pray with anyone again to receive the baptism in the Holy Spirit. Again I was playing into the hands of Satan, who wants to shut the mouth of witnessing and ministering Christians. Praise God, Who looks on the heart and Who knew that the deepest desire of my heart, and of Bob's, was still to bring others into a closer relationship with Christ! Every time we reached the point of giving up completely, the Lord would send someone to us with words of encouragement.

"When It Rains It Pours"

Bob speaking:

In November, 1970, Ruth and I took part in a three-day Charismatic Clinic at St. Martin's Episcopal Church in Saint Louis. My strength was spent after the final day of the clinic. That night I awoke with a start and with the realization that my heart was beating like a triphammer—at least 150 beats a minute. I felt as if I were going into orbit! I woke Ruth, and we began to pray and to call on the name of Jesus. I did not seem to be able to pray effectively, and I leaned on Ruth for her strength. After about 15 or 20 minutes my heartbeat returned to normal, and we went back to sleep—but the next day I was weaker than ever.

At Ruth's insistence, I consulted a doctor, who found me to be anemic but couldn't find the cause. He put me in the hospital for numerous blood tests and x-rays, but these gave no indication of what was wrong. Finally, he advised me to go to a blood specialist, since he could do no more himself. As I shared with Ruth what my doctor had said about going to a specialist, I was convicted of the fact that I was telling others about the power of God to heal, while I was putting *my* trust in doctors. Ruth and I agreed to trust God for the healing, and to leave the outcome in His hands.

We didn't think things could get much worse, but we were wrong! Our son, Steve, who had married the previous year, informed us just a few weeks after the birth of their baby girl that his marriage had broken up. What a blow this was to us, coming so shortly after the thrill of having our first grandchild! We cried out, "Oh, God, how much more can we take?" We learned (the hard way) that we could take a good deal more.

The next blow came just a few weeks later, in a letter from a well-meaning Christian friend. The tone of the letter seemed to indicate that I was very much out of God's will, and the writer suggested that I should dissolve the ministry and seek secular employment. This letter almost broke our hearts. We told God that we were willing to give up our work for Him if this was His desire, but we asked Him to confirm it out of the mouth of two or three witnesses [Deuteronomy 19:15; Matthew 18:16].

As a final blow, the house we were living in was sold, and we were told that we would have to move before January 1. Rents were very high and rental homes hard to find. It wasn't until 10 o'clock on the morning of December 31 that we found another house—in a part of town that was probably one of the last places we would have chosen. With the help of friends and relatives, we managed to move into our new home in time to greet the New Year—but not very joyfully!

The move to this undesirable location seemed to me to be the last straw. I was tired of waiting for God to answer our prayers for guidance, and I decided I was going to get a job! Within a week I had found one and was scheduled to go to Chicago for training. After talking it over, however, Ruth and I both began to feel uneasy about this decision. Deep down, I somehow knew this was not what God wanted.

I was to leave for Chicago on Sunday afternoon, and we prayed that God would block the trip if I was not to take the job. By Saturday night I was flat on my back with a high fever. On Monday, I called the company that had hired me and told them I could not accept the position. For the first time in months, we felt a peace in our hearts and knew that we were to trust God completely.

"At the Mouth of Two or Three Witnesses"

Ruth speaking:

After we were settled in our latest home, I read Merlin Carothers' book, *Prison to Praise*, and began to learn the victory that comes when we praise God even for adverse circumstances. As I began praising Him for bringing us to this town that had everything I had never wanted, the joy of the Lord began to return to my heart, bringing with it renewed strength and faith.

A few weeks later Bob and I visited a Pentecostal Church where an out-of-town evangelist was holding a meeting. In the middle of her message, the evangelist stopped, turned to the pastor, and asked him our names. Then she called us up from the congregation, saying that God had pointed us out to her. Looking Bob in the eye, she said, "Brother, the Lord told me to call you both up here. You are having a 'Job' experience, and God wants to minister to you." With that she laid hands on us and began to pray and prophesy. The power of God came down upon us, and His Spirit bore witness with our spirits that the words were from Him.

At the same time the pastor of the church was given a prophecy for us; but because he knew us and was somewhat aware of our situation, he was hesitant to bring it forth. Then the Lord gave him a vision to confirm the prophecy, and he shared them both with us and with the congregation. The essence of the message was that the Lord Himself had cut us back and pruned us, but that there was still life in the roots. The dead wood had to be cut away so that we might bring forth more fruit than ever before. Indeed it was a night of encouragement for us!

This same message was confirmed to us three more times from three different people in separate parts of the country. Three times we were given assurance that our ministry was to increase and that we were not aware of all God had planned for us.

In February, 1971, friends made it possible for us to return to California for a week of rest and fellowship. While there, we listened to a series of tapes by Bob Mumford on the subject of "Temptation." God spoke to us very definitely through these tapes, and I felt as if we were being brought back to life by mouth-to-mouth resuscitation! The tapes dealt with the promises, principles, problems, and provisions of God and how to appropriate these into our lives. Through these tapes God was telling us how to "quit going around and around the mountain," as Mumford put it. I had always wanted more than just having Scripture quoted at me. I wanted the "how to" also—and this is what we received from the teachings on the tapes.

Our spirits felt refreshed as we drove back to Missouri with friends from Saint Louis who had been attending a convention in Los Angeles. We praised God for all the blessings of the past week and committed ourselves anew to serving Him in *His* way, *His* time, and *His* place.

15

Deliverance

Bob speaking:

When we moved to Saint Louis in the summer of 1969, we had come with a wrong attitude in our hearts. We thought Saint Louis needed us; but the experience of the past year and a half had shown us that *we* needed Saint Louis so that God could perfect certain areas of our lives. For most of this time the Lord had kept us on a shelf, waiting until we were, "willing to be willing." I praise God for His love and for His wisdom in keeping our ministry here not too active until we grasped what He was saying to us.

As God put us through His school of the Spirit, He was often testing our willingness to yield to Him. When we were able to yield completely, the training period was usually over, for a time. God must have seen that Ruth and I had reached the point of real surrender when I gave up the job I had found. From that point on, things began to improve. The week in California was balm to our wounded spirits; and when we returned to Saint Louis, the town looked better to us than it had when we left it. Outside ministry began to open up, and it seemed that we could see more direction for our lives. In spite of my continued weakness and anemia, I felt more optimistic than I had in many months since moving to Saint Louis.

I began to realize that the Lord was using the weakness of my body to correct things in my life that were still displeasing to Him. I don't think He made me sick, but I believe He allowed Satan to do it. During this time of illness I repented of many sins that had crept back into my life and I saw areas change as I yielded to the Holy Spirit.

As I was going through this period of soul-searching, the Holy Spirit brought to my mind a remark I had made while Ruth and I were ministering together at a home prayer meeting in Fort Collins, Colorado. One of the men present was given a prophecy for Ruth and me, which indicated that healing was going to be added to our ministry. The prophecy was directed more to Ruth than to me; and as some of us were talking afterwards, one of the men said to me, "Maybe Ruth is going to travel by herself, and you will be taking care of the home." My reply was, "Over my dead body!" Remembering this remark after the sickness came upon me, I asked God to forgive me for it and told Him that if He wanted to do it this way, I was willing. This experience made me realize for the first time how important it is to control that unruly member, the tongue [James

3:8]. The writer of Proverbs 6:2 tells us that we are snared by the words of our mouth, and our Lord told His followers that it is not what goes into the mouth but what comes out of it that defiles a man [Matthew 15:11].

The fear that struck me when my heart began racing made me realize that I was not trusting God fully. Oh yes, I was able to say that to be absent from the body is to be present with the Lord [II Corinthians 5:8]. I thought I was looking forward to living with Jesus in heaven —but suddenly I realized that I feared death. I was not sure I was *ready* to go! While I had this fear, I was still in bondage to Satan in this area.

"Wonder-working Power"

It was on a trip to Frisco, Colorado, in June of 1971 that I submitted to deliverance ministry and realized the "power of the blood." Although I had been invited to Frisco to minister, it turned out that I was ministered *unto*. Through the ministry of those who invited me, I had deliverance from my fear of death and from other fears in my life, and also from a demonic spirit that was harassing me. The group also prayed for my physical healing, and someone gave me a booklet by Maxwell Whyte called *The Power of the Blood* (Whitaker Books, 1970).

Reading this booklet on the return flight to Saint Louis, I saw that the author often spoke of "pleading the blood." I had heard this phrase many times, and it had always "turned me off." I couldn't understand why we would have to beg and plead for the blood, since the Scriptures clearly state that Jesus freely gave His life for us. In Mr. Whyte's booklet, however, I saw that the word *plead* was used in the sense of claiming as protection—as when a lawyer *pleads* or argues his client's innocence in order to win his case.

Mr. Whyte also emphasized the fact that the life of the flesh is in the blood [Leviticus 17:11]. Not only did Jesus spill His blood on Calvary's hill, but His blood is now in the Holy of Holies. Through the eternal Spirit we can still call upon and appropriate the blood of Jesus for whatever need we have. Suddenly, I realized that Satan had no right to put this sickness on me. God had used the illness to clean up certain areas of my life, but now He wanted to use it to make me realize my authority in Jesus Christ and the power in His blood!

When I returned home, I began asking God to show me how I could make this authority real in my life. I knew it had to be more than just words coming forth from me; I had to *believe in my heart* if Satan was to obey. I had yelled at Satan before, and he had only laughed in my face; so I knew God would have to make it a revelation in my heart. Immediately I could sense God bringing reality into what had been just a concept.

Another thing I began to realize was the need for bringing forth an *audible* command. In his letter to the Romans [10:9), Paul said that if we confess *with our mouth* that Jesus is Lord and believe in our hearts that God raised Him from the dead we shall be saved. On the day of Pentecost the 120 disciples, as they received the Holy Spirit, "began to *speak* with other tongues, as the Spirit gave them utterance." [Acts 2:4] There is something about *speaking forth* that changes faith to reality.

My faith was now at a peak from the revelation I had received (as God changed His Word from head knowledge to heart knowledge). I said in a loud voice, "Satan, I plead the blood of Jesus Christ against you. I command you, in the name of Jesus, to take this illness from me." As I spoke, I believed that Satan had to submit to the authority in the name and blood of Jesus, and I rested in this assurance.

Two days after my return from Colorado, I left for Dallas, where I was scheduled to hold a meeting at an Episcopal church. This church had experienced an outpouring of the Holy Spirit, and there was great interest in the Baptism of the Holy Spirit. On the first night of the session, after teaching on the Baptism and going through the Scripture on the subject, I asked if anyone wanted personal ministry. One of the first to come forward was a young woman whose baby had died in a tragic accident a year and a half earlier. She had left the child in a high chair while she went into the back yard; on returning a few minutes later, she found that the child had somehow hanged himself in the chair. Ever since this tragedy occurred, this young mother had been condemning herself for leaving the child alone—and, as a result, she was destroying herself and her marriage.

As she talked, I recognized that Satan was back of this woman's excessive guilt feelings. I told her I believed there was demonic activity that had to be reckoned with, and she agreed to submit to ministry for deliverance. Laying my hands on her head, I commanded Satan in the name of Jesus Christ to remove the demonic spirit that was harassing her. In a few seconds she exclaimed in a loud voice, "It's gone! It's gone! It went right out the top of my head!"

Then I asked this young woman if she had ever really invited Jesus to come into her life. She said she had not but that she would like to. As I led her in a prayer accepting Jesus as her Savior, I could see a change come into her face. When I asked her if she would like to receive the power of the Holy Spirit to walk this life in Christ, she replied enthusiastically in the affirmative. I read again the passage from Acts which tells how the disciples responded to the Spirit on the day of Pentecost, then I laid hands on her head once again and asked Jesus to baptize her in His Holy Spirit. As she yielded herself to God, He filled her to overflowing and she began speaking forth in another tongue. After praying this way awhile, she said, "For the first time in my life I feel set free!" As she spoke the air seemed to be charged with electricity, so powerful was the presence of the Spirit!

When the others in the room saw God move in such a dramatic way in this woman, many indicated a desire for prayer. It was after midnight before I finished ministering to all those with special needs. As I was on my way to the home where I was staying, I suddenly realized that I did not feel tired—after more than four hours of ministry. Ever since I became anemic, I had felt exhausted by a minimum amount of exertion. Now, as I felt my strength renewed, I realized that God had touched me! What faith welled up within me then! It is thrilling to see God heal someone else—but an added measure to experience the healing power of God in your own life.

The remainder of my stay in Dallas proved to be a time of powerful ministry, as God confirmed His Word with signs following [Mark 16:20]. I returned to Saint Louis with my faith strengthened and my health being restored. New fields of ministry began opening up, in Saint Louis and elsewhere; our financial situation improved; and the future looked brighter than ever before.

16

A New Anointing

Bob speaking:

A special ministry the Lord has given Ruth and me together is that of praying for others to receive the Baptism in the Holy Spirit. From what has been revealed to us from Scripture, we expect the Lord to give a new language to each one that receives the Holy Spirit. Jesus said "Out of [your] belly shall flow rivers of living water." [John 7:38] Ruth and I are not satisfied as we pray with people until the rivers are flowing! This has been a strong emphasis in our ministry, although it has been challenged many times. God has shown us that there is power, deliverance, freedom and health in having a release in tongues! Satan also recognizes the importance of this release; the Baptism in the Holy Spirit is usually not a controversial subject until the manifestation of tongues is mentioned——then the fur flies! We had already seen many persons set free through this release and were to see even more powerful times in the future.

As we continued to mature in the Spirit and

accept God's correction it became easier to submit to His desire in our lives. We found out that when we would learn our lesson of obedience, the Lord would release more power through our ministry. We had already seen God's power move through us on different occasions, and it made us want to be used more. One example of His deliverance power had occurred in January of 1970.

On a trip to Colorado, Ruth and I were invited to minister to a small prayer group in a home. One of the women present was Lucy, a Methodist, who had known the Lord for several years but felt that she was being harassed by the devil. She told us that her mother was involved in spiritualism and through a medium was directing spirit activity against her in an effort to break her faith. After hearing our testimonies, Lucy asked us to pray for her to receive the Baptism in the Holy Spirit. I laid hands on her head and prayed aloud while Ruth was praying silently. When we asked the Lord to fill her with the Holy Spirit, she began twisting her head away. In the natural, one would have thought she decided against having prayer.

I realized, through the gift of discerning of spirits (one of the nine gifts of the Holy Spirit listed by Paul in I Corinthians 12:8-10) that this was not Lucy who was resisting the Holy Spirit but a demonic spirit trying to keep her from being set free. Taking the authority that is ours as believers [Mark 16:17], I said, "Satan, in the name of Jesus Christ I bind your demon activity and loose the faith of God through this vessel!" Although I didn't know it, Ruth had been given the same revelation and was saying almost the same words silently as I was speaking. Immediately Lucy began speaking forth in gutteral sounds that were not too pleasant to hear at first. They soon changed to a beautiful, melodious language as torrents of praise to God came forth from her lips. After about 20 minutes of praising the Lord this way, she sank back in the chair and exclaimed, "I feel all clean inside!" Jesus had set another captive free!

Some months later Lucy told us that her mother wondered what had happened to her, because the spiritualist medium who had been sending the spirit activity against her previously could not get through to her now. She told us too that, when the Lord set her free, He also healed and delivered her of epilepsy which had afflicted her since she was 12 years old. She had sometimes had as many as 30 seizures in a day. Some three months after being baptized in the Holy Spirit, she was strongly impressed not to take medication for her illness. God had completely healed her of this infirmity and she has not had a seizure to this day! I believe this illness was the result of demon activity, like the case of epilepsy described in Luke 9:37-43.

Not only did God set Lucy free and heal her, He also began working on her family. Within 9 months her husband and children received the Holy Spirit. Some two years later her mother, who had been involved in spiritualism, received

Jesus as her Saviour and Baptizer in the Holy Spirit (renouncing her previous activities in the occult.) Other relatives of Lucy have received Christ in their lives and the baptism in the Holy Spirit through her testimony!

It is really important how we minister to people because they are deeply affected by us. The end result can be positive or negative according to our ministry. They can be built up or torn down by our words. (The letter kills, but the spirit gives life—II Corinthians 3:6) As we touch peoples' lives it is like throwing a stone in the middle of a pond. The impact causes a big splash and then there are many waves that are created. These waves touch other waves and on and on they go until they reach the bank. If our splash has been in the Spirit it will *positively* change peoples' lives. And the waves will have positive effects on other lives.

After we had gone through our most recent schooling, God began to release a new anointing in our ministry. Up to this time, our ministry had a main emphasis of praying for people to receive the baptism in the Holy Spirit. The Lord now began to allow healing and deliverance to be consistently manifested.

In June of 1972 Ruth, Toni and I had planned a trip to Southern California. Since I had ministered in Arizona while living in California, we planned to stop there on the way west. We were invited to stay in the home of Art and Nancye Allen and minister there on a Saturday night. On the night of the meeting, the house was packed with friends of ours and others who desired fellowship. We had a tremendous time of praise and worship to the Lord, and then Art invited Ruth and I to minister. After we had shared in testimony and teaching, we invited those who had physical needs to come forward for prayer. One of the first to respond was a man that had a curvature of the spine and also an abnormal growth on the spine.

We told him that God was giving divine back adjustments and was also lengthening limbs; that He was demonstrating this power through many ministries in this country and abroad. As the man sat down in a chair, we measured his legs, comparing one to the other. There was about ¾ of an inch difference. Continuing to kneel before him, I held his feet together, and as we prayed, the shorter leg came out even with the other leg. He could feel the presence of God as healing began. We then had him stand to his feet. As Ruth and I laid hands on his head and back the power of the Holy Spirit hit him like a bolt of lightning! He was knocked off his feet and found himself on the floor. I believe Ruth and I were as surprised as he was. I had seen people fall when they were prayed for, but couldn't quite see what purpose it served. In fact I thought sometimes the person praying had pushed the one they were praying for down. As we looked at this man, he had a startled expression on his face. His eyes were like two large saucers that seemed to say "What happened?" After sitting there a few minutes, he stood to his feet. Immediately he realized that he stood differently now. His back felt different now, and he knew God had healed him! The growth had disappeared, and his back was straightened. In fact, he had to readjust his stance as he learned to walk normally again.

As we continued to minister to others that evening, just about every one went down from the power of God. There were many physical healings, including a woman that could not turn her head because of neck and shoulder problems. Many people also received spiritual deliverance of habits they wanted to rid themselves of. Some, after seeing God move this way, requested prayer to receive the power of the Holy Spirit in their lives. It was one of those times when it was difficult to end the fellowship. God's love and power just permeated our very beings. Previous to this I had been a "Doubting Thomas" about people falling down when they were prayed for. My pet comment would be "what purpose does it serve for people to fall down?" Ruth quipped to me after the meeting, "Bob, what was the purpose for all those people falling when you prayed for them?"

Ruth speaking:

We continued on our way West with our spirits lifted! Excitement was in our hearts, and we wondered what else God had in store for us. Several meetings had been scheduled. I spoke at two women's luncheons, one in San Diego and the other at Covina, California. I asked Bob to join me and speak with me and help pray with the people. We have found an even greater release of God's power in our ministering together in unity. Both meetings lasted until almost 5 p.m., and so much happened I can't even remember it all. People were healed, delivered, set free, and many received the Holy Spirit in His fullness.

One of the many great times was in the home of a Baptist lady in Ontario one Friday night. I especially remember an older lady who had not been able to sleep well for years due to discomfort in her back. Jesus touched her back, healed her, and she slept so soundly on Saturday night that she said she missed getting up for church on Sunday morning!

At another meeting we were surprised to see our former bookkeeper from the restaurant business fiasco! He had heard we were back in the area and had also recently read a "Voice" magazine and was now seeking to know more about the Baptism in the Holy Spirit.* It was great to go to his home about 1 a.m. and pray

---

*Someone had given this man several "Voice" magazines but it was during tax return time, and he had been too busy to read them. His wife finally picked one up and it just happened to mention our names in the testimony of George Griffith, a California Highway Patrolman. That really aroused their curiosity, and so when they heard we were going to speak at a nearby meeting, they attended to find out more about all this.

When I saw this man and his wife in the meeting that night, I was grateful that we had paid off all of our financial obligations, as he also had made out our income tax returns and had been well aware of our plight during those difficult times!

for him and his wife. We had tried to witness to him at the time of our business failure while we still lived in California but couldn't quite get through. Now here we were rejoicing and praising the Lord together!

We also met with a group of Brethren in Christ in the Brubakers' home where about 40 or 50 had received the fullness of the Holy Spirit. Again we saw God move in a special and powerful way. Our friends had been praying for 10 years for an out-pouring of God's Spirit in their church and now it was happening.

It was good to visit with our two boys, Danny and David, who still live in California. Toni was enjoying being back again in California with many of her old friends. We had left our oldest son, Steve, back home in Saint Louis to "hold the fort down."

We went on to Northern California, on to the Denver area, Omaha, and then back home to St. Louis. We didn't mind coming into Missouri anymore. In fact, it felt good to be back home again to see Steve.

Epilogue:

In Everything Give Thanks

Bob speaking:

As Ruth and I look back over the past 11 years, we give thanks to God for His strength to hold on. Had we not been willing to let Him lead us through the valleys, we would have missed what He was developing in us. There are times when a person has to hang on with all his might to what he knows God has spoken to his heart. Jacob wrestled with an angel and won a blessing because he refused to "let go." As we Christians go through our trials and times of testing, we need to wrestle with the problems in the power of the Holy Spirit so that God can also give us a blessing.

Someone has said, "The brook would lose its song if you removed the stones." We Christians often want to have the stones removed from our lives before we are willing to sing our song. The real test of our trust in God is to praise Him while the stones are still making us uncomfortable. The Lord allows troubles to comes into our lives to perfect us and to help us develop our faith and trust Him.

140

Faith reaches out where reason cannot go. The Lord gives each of us a measure of faith, but its growth depends on the way we use it. Just as a seed has to be planted in the earth if it is to sprout and grow, so does our measure of faith have to be planted in our earthly circumstances if it is to increase. Jesus said, "If ye have faith as a grain of mustard seed, ye shall say unto this mountain, Remove hence to yonder place; and it shall remove." [Matthew 17:20] If you have ever held a tiny mustard seed in your hand, you can get an idea of the tremendous power of faith.

We are living in an era when problems seem to surround us on all sides—but so did the first Christians! The important thing is not how many difficulties we face, but how we face the difficulties. This is what reveals our true character. The storm brings out the eagles, but the little birds take cover. If we let Him, God uses troubles to develop Christian stamina. Paul told the Romans that "tribulation worketh patience; and patience, experience; and experience, hope; and hope maketh not ashamed; because the love of God is shed abroad in our hearts by the Holy Ghost which is given unto us." [Romans 5:3-5]

Ruth and I have had many spiritual Jerichos in our Christian walk, and we had never seen the walls come tumbling down until we had learned the dual lesson of trust (faith) and obedience. Only once did obedience entail marching around the "city" seven times and claiming

141

victory in the name of Jesus—but always trust has required giving thanks "in everything . . . : for this is the will of God in Christ Jesus concerning you." [I Thessalonians 5:18]

INSPIRATIONAL CATALOGUE
AVAILABLE

If you have enjoyed this book you may want to read other publications that are available through Banner Publishing. We have listed books on the next pages that we feel will be of interest to you. Our catalogue describes these and hundreds of other inspirational Christian books and cassette tapes.

To receive a catalogue or order any of these books, send your name and address to:

———————— DETACH HERE ————————

Banner Publishing
504 LAUREL DRIVE
MONROEVILLE, PA. 15146

Please send me a copy of your catalog.

NAME_____

ADDRESS_____

_____ZIP_____

Suggested Inspirational Paperback Books

ANOTHER WAVE ROLLS IN—Bartleman	$ .75
BAPTISM IN THE HOLY SPIRIT: COMMAND OR OPTION—Campbell	.95
CAN A CHRISTIAN HAVE A DEMON—Basham	1.25
COOKBOOK OF FOODS FROM BIBLE DAYS—McKibbin	.95
DEAR DAD, THIS IS TO ANNOUNCE MY DEATH—Kast	1.25
DOMINION OVER DEMONS—Whyte	.95
FACE UP WITH A MIRACLE—Basham	.95
FAITH IN ERUPTION—Robeson	.95
GATEWAY TO POWER—Smith	1.25
A HANDBOOK ON HOLY SPIRIT BAPTISM —Basham	.95
A HANDBOOK ON TONGUES, INTERPRE- TATION AND PROPHECY—Basham	1.25
HE SPOKE—AND I WAS STRENGTHENED—Mills	1.25
IT CAN HAPPEN TO ANYBODY!—Bixler	1.25
JESUS IS ALIVE—Stockhowe	.95
THE LAST CHAPTER—Rasmussen	1.25
LEARNING TO LIVE IN THE LOVE OF GOD—Pickerill	.95
LET GO!—Fenelon	.95
LET US MAKE MAN—Beall	1.25
LOOKING TO JESUS—Monod	.50
MINISTERING THE BAPTISM IN THE HOLY SPIRIT—Basham	1.00
ONE BODY IN CHRIST—Kurosaki	1.25
THE POWER OF THE BLOOD—Whyte	.95
THE SCHOOL OF THE HOLY SPIRIT—Beall	1.25
A SCRIPTURAL OUTLINE OF THE BAPTISM IN THE HOLY SPIRIT—Gillies	.50
SIGI AND I—Schmidt	.95
UNDERSTANDING GOD—Gruits	3.00
USING YOUR SPIRITUAL AUTHORITY— Brooks	1.25
VISIONS BEYOND THE VEIL—Baker	.95
WHAT'S YOUR QUESTION?—Sumrall	.95